DOSSIER
09

FINANCIAL
PERFORMANCE

ACKNOWLEDGEMENTS

This publication was developed by Scitech Educational in partnership with NEBS Management.

Project management:	Diana Thomas (NEBS Management)
	Don McLeod (Scitech Educational)
Series editor:	Darren O'Conor
Authors:	Jim Borland, Don McLeod

Dossier 09: Financial Performance

A Scitech Educational publication

Distributed by Scitech-DIOL

ISBN 0 948672 62 5

Published by:
Scitech Educational Ltd
15 – 17 The St John Business Centre
St Peter's Road
Margate
Kent CT9 1TE
United Kingdom

Tel:	+44 (0)1843 234740
Fax:	+44 (0)1843 231485
Website:	www.universal-manager.co.uk
	www.scitechdiol.co.uk

CONTENTS

FINANCIAL PERFORMANCE

THE UNIVERSAL MANAGER SERIES

Books

01 Risk Management
02 Delivering Successful Projects
03 Planning and Controlling Projects
04 The Learning Organization
05 Managing for Knowledge
06 Obtaining and Retaining Customers
07 Human Resource Planning
08 Business Planning
09 Financial Performance
10 Managing Quality
11 Business Relationships
12 Managing for High Performance
13 Managing Harmoniously
14 21st Century Communication
15 Managing for Sustainability

Computer-based Resources

Management Assignments (CD-ROM)
Personal Development Planning Toolkit
 (at www.universal-manager.co.uk)
Learning Styles Toolkit
 (at www.universal-manager.co.uk)

PREFACE

As world markets are becoming rationalized and more mature, the traditionally rich Western countries see the economies of the Far East growing extremely rapidly and closing the gap in many areas such as technology, skills base, knowledge base and so on. Consequently, the Western economies are coming under pressure to maintain their relative standard of living. And although political consensus on global trade eludes the politicians of the world (as in the failed GATT talks), barriers to global trade are being swept aside by multinational corporations who are well placed to exploit the advances in communications and technology. Globalization has developed in the last half of the twentieth century to the extent that the overwhelming majority of organizations today are unlikely to remain isolated from international economic pressures by sheltering behind the nation state.

The winners in this maelstrom of change are the global corporations — those that run their own banking systems and hence control their own international cash flows. They can dictate to governments the conditions on which they will establish business units in one territory or another, and can fund the development of teams of international executives without local responsibility.

Potential losers are small and medium sized enterprises that are geographically or financially constrained, and public sector organizations at local, regional and national level. These groups will feel, more than any others, the financial consequences of increasing global competitiveness. Quite apart from the direct competition between enterprises in far-flung countries, governments in Western economies find themselves less able to fund the state infrastructure and machinery they inherited from the mid-twentieth century. Through public–private partnerships, national governments now seek new ways to raise money and decrease their contribution, in an effort to fund the spiralling costs of the executive, the legislature, defence and health care services.

Actual losers are those organizations, in whatever sector, who are not able to manage their finances astutely — astute financial management does not necessarily mean employing a superb set of accountants to run the organization's finances, or paying for the advice of a global consultancy firm. It means that managers at all levels (if levels still remain) have to be attuned to the financial consequences of their acts and omissions. They must have the freedom to commit resources rapidly to back up their well-informed decisions.

The revolution in information and communications technology (ICT) is perhaps the greatest aid to financial modelling and decision taking. An example of the benefits of the technological revolution are the inexpensive and widely available ICT systems that can support:

- Communication in a flat organizational structure
- Rapid transfer of funds
- Detailed financial planning and analysis
- Control systems for widely delegated budgets.

These systems exist for organizations to exploit.

In his *Circle of Innovation* (Coronet, 1999) Tom Peters cites the example of a hotel chain in the USA where all staff, including the lowliest porter and chambermaid, could commit up to $2,000 of organization funds to deliver an immediate solution for any customer's problem, if it was judged necessary. Apart from the sheer courage of the management team involved and the innovative approach to customer care, this clearly would not work if there were not monitoring and control systems, training and teamwork firmly in place. Financial crises would be inevitable if the hotel chain, say, had fifty hotels all employing 100 staff, 10% of whom used this facility to its full extent once a month! The integration of financial management into planning, marketing and operations is clearly essential in such decisions.

In other words, tomorrow belongs to the organization whose managers are able to seize the opportunities afforded by, for example:

- Globalization (e.g. reducing costs by sourcing less costly components from another country).
- ICT (e.g. using the internet to carry out rapid competitive analysis to make price or margin alterations, or to deliver a budget forecast quickly via e-mail to a person compiling the master budget on the other side of the world).
- Small size (e.g. similar marketing opportunities are available on the internet to small companies as to large companies).

The need for financial discipline in this environment is far greater today than it was in the relatively slow-moving world of the twentieth century. And because distributing and obtaining financial information is now so easy and rapid (with consequent challenges for managers and decision-making processes), there is an ever greater need for an ethical approach to financial management. There are now many more ways, for example, in which a group of organizations can exchange financial data and hence operate a sophisticated cartel beyond the reach of national governments.

This dossier introduces some of the ideas essential to managing with financial discipline. These ideas are essential because to attempt to manage today without an understanding of them would be like attempting to sculpt a bronze purely in one dimension. Planning, decision-making, communicating within and outside the organization, and delivering excellent service would all be impaired without an understanding of financial management. It was possible in the old days when managers' main task was to control information — but it's not like that any more.

www.universal-manager.co.uk

LEARNING PROFILE

Topics included in this dossier are listed below. Use them to make a quick judgement about the level of your current knowledge and understanding, and to highlight the sections of the dossier which will be most useful to you.

KEY	Low	You have never or not recently studied this topic, nor recently applied the concepts at work.
	Mid	You have a broad understanding of the concepts or some experience of working with them, but are not confident about your current level of knowledge.
	High	You are familiar with the concepts and their theoretical underpinning. You could confidently apply the concepts in any work context.

	Low	Mid	High
(1) Accounting Methods and Financial Analysis			
☛ Distinctions between management and financial accounting	❑	❑	❑
☛ The importance of effective processes and practices for financial communication	❑	❑	❑
☛ Financial standards and the role of auditors in enforcing them	❑	❑	❑
☛ The cross-over between financial and ethical business policies and practices	❑	❑	❑
☛ Key financial reports: Profit & loss, the Balance Sheet	❑	❑	❑
☛ Approaches to asset valuation and depreciation	❑	❑	❑
☛ The use of ratios to quantify liquidity, profitability, activity and debt	❑	❑	❑
(2) Forecasting Techniques			
☛ The fit between corporate strategy and financial forecasts	❑	❑	❑
☛ Techniques for analysing the business climate and environment: SWOT, STEEP and competitive forces analysis	❑	❑	❑
☛ Techniques for forecasting financial requirements	❑	❑	❑
☛ Investment appraisal methods: Return on Capital, Payback and Discounted Cash Flow	❑	❑	❑
(3) Managing Budgets			
☛ Characteristics and benefits of effective budgeting processes	❑	❑	❑
☛ Budget preparation methods and cycles	❑	❑	❑
☛ Preparing the master budget	❑	❑	❑
☛ Budgeting methods: forecast, flexible, zero-based and capital budgeting	❑	❑	❑
(4) Costing Techniques			
☛ Functional costs: direct and indirect	❑	❑	❑
☛ Behavioural costs: fixed, variable and semi-variable	❑	❑	❑
☛ Control classification: controllable and non-controllable costs	❑	❑	❑
☛ Techniques for costing future activity	❑	❑	❑
☛ The value chain and its contribution to cost control	❑	❑	❑

Financial Performance

(5) Cash Management

☛ Profiling working capital	❏	❏	❏
☛ Methods for controlling credit and stock	❏	❏	❏
☛ Calculating profit margins	❏	❏	❏
☛ Analysis of the organization's capital gearing	❏	❏	❏
☛ Accounting for taxation: corporation tax, VAT, PAYE and NIC	❏	❏	❏
☛ Understanding shareholder motivation	❏	❏	❏
☛ Key ratios for analysis of share value: earnings per share, price earnings, dividend yield	❏	❏	❏
☛ Planning capital expenditure	❏	❏	❏

www.universal-manager.co.uk

09-1 ACCOUNTING METHODS AND FINANCIAL ANALYSIS

09-1 ACCOUNTING METHODS AND FINANCIAL ANALYSIS

'Accountants are the witch-doctors of the modern world and are willing to turn their hands to any kind of magic.'
(Lord Justice Harman, 1964)

 ## 09-1-1 Management versus Financial Accounting

The Need for Clear Communication

There are substantial differences between the two main schools of management accounting and financial accounting, and the roles played by each method should be complementary. As with any successful aspect of business activity, the need for clear and integrated communications systems is essential to ensure that the two roles support each other.

Financial and managerial accounts are simply tools to be utilized by managers in a decision making process. It is the responsibility of those who practise accountancy to make a serious study of the communication processes within an organizational setting. Since poor communication is frequently the barrier between financial and management accountants, the following overview of the process of communication is included to demonstrate the need for a coherent communication ethos as part of the proper development of organizational success.

The process of communication comprises the following constituent parts:

(1)   The communication sender

The communication sender is the person who has the knowledge, ability and intention to send a particular message, in this context the organizational accountant.

(2)   The communication receiver(s)

The receiver or receivers will be the target audience for the communication sender. Many of these receivers may not be accountants, but could be councillors, voluntary workers, retail managers or production managers, for example.

(3)   The reason behind the communication

In any organization, the reason or purpose of the communication should be for the future benefit of the organization. The reason will be the intent in the mind of the sender; the sender must therefore ensure that the language used is acceptable to those receiving it.

(4)   The communication substance

The content of the message may concern planning, financial problems, the adoption of new methods of recording data, or any other aspect of financial information.

(5)   The communication method

The method chosen by the sender may reflect the urgency, detail and feedback requirements of the sender. The methods may include:

☛   Telephone, fax, or e-mail
☛   Memoranda, letter or financial report
☛   Face-to-face meetings.

(6)   The communication environment

The chosen environment can influence the interpretation of the communication. For example, the communication might take place in an environment such as a council meeting, or could occur in the office of the marketing manager, or might take place on the shop floor of a production organization.

Financial Performance

Although communication with colleagues, customers or shareholders should be straightforward, it is essential that the sender should anticipate any potential problems that might affect the receipt and acceptance of the message that is to be sent. In financial management, problem areas in the process of communication include the following:

☛ *Physical Environment*

Self-evidently the situation where the communication is being sent/received.

☛ *Disposition of receiver/sender*

Again, self-evidently the disposition of both the sender and the receiver may affect the way the message is communicated. E-mail is particularly susceptible to being affected in this way since it is an 'instant' medium. Like 'live' communication such as meetings (except video conferencing) and the phone, feelings and emotions can become integrated into the communication. However, unlike 'live' communications, e-mail writers are often less inhibited — the conventions (of hierarchy and society) are either absent or less constraining. Consider the potential for differences, for example, between sending/receiving a 'tough' cash flow forecast on a hard copy printout accompanied by a letter, and the same forecast sent/received electronically in a spreadsheet attached to an e-mail.

☛ *Attitude*

It is not our purpose to explore the complexities of the way in which attitudes affect communication. It is worth noting that attitudes can be reflected in financial figures, just like any other message. On the one hand, an optimistic revenue forecast might be a function of a 'sender' who is:

☛ Naturally optimistic — may (or may not) be removed from the facts
☛ Subservient — someone who wants to produce what the boss wants irrespective of reality
☛ Stressed — produces the right figures in the hope that the pressure will go away
☛ Inept — the person is out of touch with the facts.

On the other hand, figures can be interpreted by a 'receiver' in a number of different ways. Consider the example of a salesman who has sold an item for £100. It cost £50 in the first place, so he says 'We made 100% profit'. The accountant disagrees and says 'No you didn't. If it cost £50 and you only sold it for £100, your profit is really 50%.' The salesman naturally wants to see his figures in the best possible light, and the accountant wants to be as realistic as possible. Actually, neither of them is completely wrong, and neither is completely right, which brings us to the final point about communication in managing financial performance.

www.universal-manager.co.uk

☞ *Jargon*

Like any of the disciplines within management such as knowledge management, project management, quality management, and so on, financial management has its own terminology. If we use the terminology casually, it becomes jargon. This is fine if two or more people have the same level of understanding of the terminology — jargon can make for more efficient teamworking. Problems arise where the jargon is used:

09-1

- ☞ Carelessly — without appreciating the different levels of understanding
- ☞ To gain advantage — to create the perception of differences between the sender and receiver, usually that one is more knowledgeable than the other.

If we look at the earlier example of the salesman and the accountant, they are both guilty of using the word 'profit' carelessly. (We will give them the benefit of the doubt!) Actually, what the salesman should have said was something like 'We sold at 100% mark-up.' And the accountant should have said something like 'That gives us a gross margin of 50%'. The example begs the question as to whether the salesman is 'profit aware'. In other words, are his targets based on profit or turnover? This is a judgement for managers, but the old saying should be borne in mind:

'Turnover is vanity.
Profit is sanity.'

Finally, it must be borne in mind that financial management can be conducted more effectively if all concerned communicate properly. This will mean that where budgets, profit targets or cost targets are delegated, appropriate financial training must be given to the budget holders or those responsible for achieving targets. It is important that the training is appropriate — the holder of a small purchasing budget in a department of a large organization would not need to understand how to conduct ratio analyses of balance sheets.

09-1-2   The Background to Financial Accounting

Financial accounting for the most part is concerned with the accurate recording and computing of the various financial transactions of an organization over a period of time. This time period is generally a year. However the year chosen can be a calendar year, a financial, tax or fiscal year (April – March) or in some instances a trading year which can have any month as a start point. For example, a football club may have the start date for its trading year at the commencement of a new football season, i.e. August – July.

The financial accounts of an organization must adhere to accepted accounting standards and practices, and will be subjected to auditing procedures to ensure their probity. The following section briefly considers the essential role played by auditors in ensuring that financial standards are met and maintained, that organizations realize their social responsibilities, and that the increasing moves toward globalization are properly considered in a framework of ethical financial planning.

Auditing

The current definition of an audit given in the *Concise Guide to Auditing Standards and Guidelines* is as follows:

> 'The independent examination of, and expression of opinion on, the financial statements of an enterprise.'

The process of auditing is becoming increasingly difficult as auditors are called upon to develop a wide and important skills base including:

☞ Financial accounting methodology

☞ Auditing processes and procedures

☞ Information technology and computing

☞ Statistical inference

☞ Communication processes.

Auditing plays an important role, more so as corporate organizations evolve due to:

☞ The increasing size of organizations, especially in the business sector

☞ The move toward globalization in business

☞ The technologically driven increase in organizational complexity

☞ The more demanding socioeconomic and legislative frameworks in the European Union

☞ The increasing political pressures for corporations to be cognizant of their social responsibility in the provision of accurate and correct financial information

☞ The social and political demands for organizations to develop their sense of ethical responsibility.

The owners, directors and managers of any organization must be fully aware of their responsibility to their stakeholders. It is the duty of auditors to support directors in this activity through the preparation of the accounts of the organization in a responsible fashion. Stakeholders will include any or all of the following:

☞ Shareholders
☞ Local authorities
☞ Employees
☞ Customers/clients
☞ The general public
☞ Suppliers
☞ Lending institutions.

Financial Performance

This kind of financial reporting is aimed at the 'outside' world, including shareholders. It needs auditing rules because of the division of ownership and control.

ACTIVITY 1

(1) Looking at your own organization, make a list of the stakeholders and rank them in order of their influence on the way the business is run.

(2) Do you think that the balance is right, i.e. does one group have too much influence, is one group under-represented, and so on?

(3) If the balance is not 'right', what strategies for change would you recommend?

(4) Is the interest of each stakeholder group monetary, political or something else?

Now read on.

www.universal-manager.co.uk

Due to the inherent difficulties in the task of auditing, auditors are required to maintain the highest possible standards of financial probity in the UK. The Consultative Committee of Accounting Bodies (CCAB) sets the definition of auditing standards which are implemented and monitored through the Financial Reporting Council (FRC).

The underpinning values pursued by the Association of Auditors for the practice of auditing are:

☛   The presentation of truth and fairness
☛   The requirement of financial evidence
☛   The need for the auditor to be truly independent
☛   The requirement for clear responsibility in carrying out the auditor's duty.

CASE STUDY:
HOTHFIELD ENGINEERING LTD

As an example, consider the case of Hothfield Engineering Ltd — a manufacturer supplying moulds to the plastics industry. It is a small, high precision engineering business turning over about £10M a year based on the sale of a relatively small number of high-value metal moulds. Imagine that the directors decided to develop a new style of mould based on a revolutionary new alloy. It is not a product they are being asked for by their customers — the plastics companies — but it is a product that the directors of Hothfield Engineering feel offers such advantages that their customers will want to buy into it. The directors decide to invest in the development of some trial products at a cost of £250,000. Their anticipated net profit for the year is £750,000 but they do not think that this important investment should be treated as a direct cost to the profit & loss account. They decide to capitalize the development cost of £250,000 as they would with the purchase of a new CAD/CAM machine.

At the end of the financial year, the auditors carry out their usual work with Hothfield Engineering, checking and sampling the audit trails, particularly of the main items such as salaries, tax, plant capitalization and depreciation, and so on. They are concerned, however, about the capitalization of the £250,000 spent on the new product development. They request a meeting with the directors for an explanation of this significant item.

The duty of the auditors is to satisfy themselves that their auditing of Hothfield Engineering's accounts is in accordance with Standard Accounting Procedures and they therefore ask the directors to explain:

- What is the definition of this development project?
- How are the development costs accounted for?
- Where are the audit trails to support this?
- Who are the anticipated customers for the new products?
- What is the anticipated additional revenue from the new products over the next few years?
- What are the directors' proposals for depreciating this capitalized development cost?

The auditors then have the task of deciding if the directors' explanations are reasonable given the auditors' knowledge of Hothfield Engineering, its customers and other businesses.

If auditors judge that a firm's directors are able to provide the audit trails to substantiate their actions, and that these are reasonable in the broader business context, then the auditors will find their task relatively straightforward. If, however, they see a declining asset base within an organization, a shortage of cash, and/or directors eager to manipulate figures to justify dividend payouts or bonuses, then auditors will have the difficult task of advising the directors of their fiduciary responsibilities and the requirements of a rigorous audit. Ultimately, the auditors can 'qualify the accounts' or even more seriously, resign. Either step would send a warning signal to an organization's stakeholders that something is seriously wrong with the financial management of the organization.

Accounting Standards

In the UK the accounting standards are referred to as SSAPs (Statements of Standard Accounting Practice) and in the USA, GAAP (Generally Accepted Accounting Principles). The previous section underlined the need for a professional approach to auditing and the overarching role in the UK of the CCAB in relation to auditing standards. The same body directs standards in accounting practice through the Accounting Standards Committee, established in 1970.

The major areas of remit of the ASC are as follows:

☞ The fundamental aspects of financial accounting

☞ A clear and unambiguous definition of financial terms to be used

☞ Recognition of the existence of different types of organizations and classes of business, and the ways in which the fundamentals of financial accounting can be applied to these different organizations

☞ The form in which financial statements should be presented

☞ The content of financial statements

☞ The requirements of financial statement disclosure.

In 1990, three bodies were established to further develop the role of standard setting for companies in the business sector. These were the Financial Reporting Council (FRC), the Accounting Standards Board (ASB), and the Review Panel. Although the major directives concerning standards in financial management are the SSAPs, these are prescriptive only to organizations in the private sector, and to all intents and purposes, they are simply guidelines to organizations in the public sector.

Social Responsibility of Organizations

As recognition grows among corporate organizations that a pursuit of profit alone is unlikely to maintain their competitive position, socially responsible policies are emerging which sometimes place unusual demands on financial accountants. Treating financial accounts within the context of a profit & loss account is relatively straightforward, but what accounting policies and practices should be applied to, for example, a conservation policy? Ultimately commercial organizations are in the business of generating profits, so the role of the financial accountant becomes central to the financial backdrop of implementing these policies.

PAUSE TO REFLECT

Does your organization operate 'environmentally friendly' policies? Or does it have a policy towards the local community? What is the cost to the organization of such policies? Are they worth it?

Typical policies might include some of the following (not forgetting that the overall aim is to generate profit):

(1)   Policies of economic growth and efficiency

This may seem an obvious business policy but it can be carried through with clear social responsibility, for example:

- ☛ Ensuring employment prospects in the areas in which the organization is situated
- ☛ Using research and development to pursue innovation, thus ensuring continuity of employment opportunities
- ☛ Establishing a policy of price control to optimize, rather than maximize, profits
- ☛ Re-investing profit to enable survival, stability, and growth policies to be pursued
- ☛ Providing support for Government social reform measures through improved organization/governmental liaison
- ☛ Improving the health of workers through organization medical care programmes
- ☛ Establishing health centres within the community to improve community health.

(2)   Policies to assist the development of educational opportunity

With a clear policy on developing the community alongside the organization, many companies will involve themselves with educational establishments, for example:

- ☛ Establishing research chairs at universities
- ☛ Allowing employees to become school or college governors
- ☛ Providing equipment for educational establishments.

(3)   Policies to assist disadvantaged groups in society

Many social awareness policies can revolve around the employment and training policies followed by the organization. For example, in the UK, DIY retailer B & Q followed a policy in the 1990s of employing the over 50s, as they had been identified as a group in whom traditional values such as loyalty and hard work were embedded. Other groupings could include:

- ☛ Women returners
- ☛ Ethnic minorities
- ☛ People with disabilities.

www.universal-manager.co.uk

(4) Policies aimed at urban renewal and development

Where Government and business combine to utilize 'brown-field sites', a common denominator for both might be to remove urban blight through:

- ☞ The joint development of low-cost housing
- ☞ The establishment of out-of-town shopping centres such as Bluewater near Dartford in Kent
- ☞ The improvement of transportation infrastructure
- ☞ The redevelopment of city centres, such as Trafford in Manchester.

(5) Policies to encourage conservation and recreation

Again, when organizations seek to establish an operation within an area of outstanding natural beauty, the costs of integration with the environment and the acceptance of environmentally friendly policies must be considered, for example:

- ☞ Preserving recreational areas
- ☞ Protecting wildlife
- ☞ Preserving flora
- ☞ Developing sports facilities
- ☞ Landscaping
- ☞ Pollution control
- ☞ Recycling.

(6) Policies which support culture and the arts

As with policies concerning the environment and education, any organization has a social role to play in the encouragement of culture and the arts, through policies such as:

- ☞ Giving financial support and advice
- ☞ Sponsorship deals.

Financial justification might be through marketing or through the encouragement of an environment of creativity and innovation.

 **ACTIVITY 2**

(1) In the last activity, you considered the stakeholders in your own organization — who they were, their interests and so on. How would the main stakeholder groups respond if:

☛ There was a marked decline in financial performance, e.g. a net loss reported, dividends reduced/stopped, a significant cash deficit reported, etc.?

☛ There was a marked improvement in financial performance, e.g. a greatly improved net profit reported, dividends increased, a significant cash surplus reported, etc.?

(2) What would the impact of their response be on any social policies of the organization in the short and medium term?

Now read on.

 09-1-3   Trading and Profit & Loss Accounts and Balance Sheets

Financial accounting also produces the various final accounts which are produced by a process of bookkeeping, through books of prime entry, ledgers and other records. They work to a system of double entry in which each transaction is recorded twice, i.e. every credit entry has a corresponding debit entry. This is the basic function of bookkeeping from which ledgers and books are balanced to prepare the Trial Balance. It is from the trial balance that the major 'Final Accounts' of the organization are prepared.

Financial accounting is the consideration of the historic measurement of the income and expenditure of an organization and the proper recording of the assets and liabilities accrued by the organization over time.

In this section, the major final accounts that will be examined in detail are:

☞ The Trading and Profit & Loss Account

☞ The Balance Sheet.

As previously discussed, the financial probity of an organization is developed within a framework of standards, checks and balances. However, it comes as no surprise (especially where money is concerned) that practice and theory do not necessarily equate, and several financial loop-holes have been identified concerning corporate financial recording. To address these issues, the Cadbury Committee was established in the UK to further improve financial reporting.

The Cadbury Report 1992

In the 1980s several high-profile public limited companies had been less than honest brokers with regard to the reporting of their financial dealings. The Cadbury Committee was established to examine the veracity of corporate financial reporting. The major theme of their remit was to consider current standards and practices, and the way in which organizations should implement these.

In 1992 the report of the Cadbury Committee was published. It contained exemplars of best practice concerning the publication of the various financial documents of an organization intended for public consumption. The report underlined the responsibility of directors to ensure that financial reports from their organization were able to withstand any required external scrutiny. Some of the recommendations made were as follows:

☞ That financial documents should be readily understandable

☞ That the external and internal control methods should be advised, such as a strict adherence to auditing procedures.

It is incumbent upon the senior management of any organization to ensure that public documents are prepared with the utmost probity. The Cadbury Report emphasized in specific terms that those employees who are of director status within an organization are in a clear and responsible position based on a fiduciary relationship between an agent (the director) and a principal (the employing organization). The whole basis of a fiduciary relationship is one of trust.

Financial Performance

Other responsibilities that rest with directors of an organization are to:

- ☞ Ensure that the organization is properly managed
- ☞ Ensure that all assets are properly safeguarded
- ☞ Keep books of accounts and ensure proper accounting records are kept
- ☞ Produce a profit & loss account and balance sheet in such a fashion as to show a true and fair view of organizational financial activity
- ☞ Produce a directors' report which shows consistency with the major financial statements.

CASE STUDY: RAINDROP PLC (1)

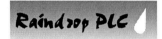

The following summarized accounts of Raindrop PLC show the two most commonly prepared final accounts used by organizations to indicate the performance of the organization, in financial terms, over a period of time — usually one year.

These final accounts are:

- ☞ The trading and profit & loss account
- ☞ The balance sheet.

The summarized financial information for Raindrop PLC, for the period 1997 to 1999, is shown below.

Note: This data will be referred to throughout this section.

TRADING AND PROFIT & LOSS ACCOUNTS			
	1997 £000s	1998 £000s	1999 £000s
Sales	2624	2899	3666
Costs of Sales	1862	1924	2042
Gross Profit	**762**	**975**	**1624**
Expenses			
Salaries	360	360	484
Advertising	125	130	282
Administration	45	55	85
Net Profit	**232**	**430**	**773**

www.universal-manager.co.uk

BALANCE SHEET AS AT 31 DECEMBER

	1997 £000s	1998 £000s	1999 £000s
Fixed Assets			
Land & buildings	2456	2988	4287
Vehicles	866	1026	1158
Total Fixed Assets	**3322**	**4014**	**5445**
Current Assets			
Cash and bank	246	368	664
Debtors	520	683	892
Stock	682	792	925
Pre-payments	86	98	104
Total Current Assets	**1534**	**1941**	**2585**
Total Assets (Fixed & Current)	**4856**	**5955**	**8030**
Current Liabilities			
Creditors	148	286	494
Bank overdraft	68	89	288
Dividends	180	180	240
Taxation	114	128	146
Total Current Liabilities	**510**	**683**	**1168**
Long-term Liabilities			
Debentures	400	400	400
Total Liabilities	**910**	**1083**	**1568**
Total Net Assets	**3946**	**4872**	**6462**
FINANCED BY			
Share capital			
(£1 shares fully paid)	3000	3600	4800
Retained earnings	946	1272	1662
	3946	**4872**	**6462**

09-1

The Trading and Profit & Loss Account

The salient features of this account are the computations used to calculate the various profits (or losses) made by the organization during a financial period. Two main profits are calculated:

☛ Gross Profit

☛ Net Profit.

The gross profit is calculated by simply subtracting the cost of goods sold from the organization's turnover or sales figure. The net profit is the profit made by the organization after all expenses associated with turnover have been paid. In essence, net profit is the gross profit figure minus expenses such as administration and marketing costs, etc.

The culture of an organization will encompass those aspects that will contribute toward the ethos, morals, and character of the organization, and these will influence the policies adopted and strategies pursued by the organization, particularly the way in which it views/reports profits (or losses). In business there are two basic philosophies concerning corporate profit, and both can provide good arguments to substantiate their specific view:

☛ Profit maximization

☛ Social conscience.

The first of these is a philosophy developed by Professor Milton Friedman which advocates the stance of profit maximization. This position is backed by the following arguments:

☛ Profit maximization is the fiduciary duty of directors in their role as agents of a principal.

☛ Profit maximization is the duty of an organizational manager to increase the wealth of the owners.

☛ Each individual within an organization will have different sets of beliefs and values, and a successful and profitable concern can assist us to do our ethical duty as individuals.

☛ Meeting the needs of society is a role for elected government and not of business.

The second of these philosophies takes a different stance in its attitude to social conscience and provision.

This philosophy is based on the organizational priority of helping to meet the needs of society. In this case, corporate management has to balance the need of the organization to remain profitable with social need. The basic precept of this philosophy is that of profit optimization (to generate the best possible profit given the social agenda) rather than profit maximization (where to make the most profit is the overriding priority). This philosophy is a characteristic of organizations in the voluntary sector and other not-for-profit organizations. Distinctions can become blurred in some not-for-profit organizations for two reasons:

☞ Strategic decisions can become emotional rather than rational
☞ Not-for-profit organizations can be used for tax avoidance.

A typical mechanism to manage the natural tension between the profit and social agendas is found in the UK where a charity, for example, can establish a trading organization. The managers of the trading organization are free to pursue a commercial, profit-generating strategy. In parallel, the trustees of the charity obtain revenue from the profits of the trading organization, and deploy the revenue to meet the requirements of the charity's social agenda. (There are complex rules and regulations surrounding these areas of corporate, trust, tax and charity law.)

The Balance Sheet

The corporate balance sheet is a summary statement of the financial position of an organization at a given period of time, such as at the conclusion of a trading period. This is why the short phrase 'as at' is usually seen at the top of a balance sheet, e.g. 'as at 31 December 1999'.

The major parts of the balance sheet comprise a listing of:

☞ Assets
☞ Liabilities
☞ The way in which these have been financed.

Assets, Valuation and Depreciation

The assets of an organization are considered in two categories:

- ☞ Fixed assets such as land, buildings, vehicles and furniture (long term assets)
- ☞ Current assets including, cash, bank balances, debtors and stock (inventory).

An important consideration in respect of assets is the way in which these assets are given a specific value on the organizational balance sheet. The assets are shown at a value which is consistent with the assumptions and conventions adopted for preparing the financial statements. The valuation is objective, can be confirmed by evidence, and is consistent with the principles of true and fair presentation.

As there is no prescribed single way in which assets are valued, there are a number of acceptable methods of recording asset value which meet the criteria of 'true and fair presentation'.

It should be noted at this stage that the main category of valuation of assets is that of fixed assets. However, in the current asset category, stock or inventory will also need to conform to an asset valuation methodology.

The most used methods of asset valuation are based on the notion of historical cost which means that the assets are valued within the balance sheet at the price paid for them. Historical cost can create some anomalies within the recording of asset values, as the same item purchased in different economic quantities, or purchased from different suppliers, or purchased in different time periods, will have different values to show. This problem can be further compounded by depreciation, an area to be considered later.

Two other often-quoted methods of asset valuation are net book value and gross book value. Both methods have their roots in historic cost valuation, and their difference is simply that net book value is adjusted to take into account depreciation, whereas gross book value considers the asset value and does not include a factor for depreciation.

To consider asset valuation and attempt to obtain values that are meaningful and consider replacement costs, some organizations show their asset base at current value, which not only considers the present or current price of the asset, but also outlines the potential opportunity cost of replacing such an asset.

Accounting Methods and Financial Analysis

As previously mentioned, an accounting convention referred to as 'depreciation' is also considered in asset valuation, especially in the area of fixed asset valuation, but generally excluding the value of land and buildings, which may show an adjustment for appreciation.

The two most widely used methods of depreciation are:

- Straight line depreciation
- Reducing balance depreciation.

Straight line depreciation is based on the following formula:

$$D = \frac{C - S}{L}$$

Where:

D = the annual depreciation charge.
C = the original cost of the asset.
S = the expected resale value at the end of the asset's useful life, although reselling of this type is rarely used in practice.
L = length of time.

Reducing balance depreciation is calculated by allocating a depreciation percentage to the year-on-year reducing asset value. For example, if the fixed asset for Raindrop PLC in 1999 is subjected to depreciation for the future the following situations could appear:

Using the Straight Line Method

Raindrop PLC

Fixed Assets

Vehicles:
$$D = \frac{C - S}{L} =$$

$$\frac{£1,158,000 - £158,000}{5} = £200,000$$

The depreciation of Raindrop's fixed assets will be calculated as £200,000 per annum over five years, using the straight line method.

Using the Reducing Balance Method

As mentioned previously, this method is based on the allocation of a percentage depreciation, which is constant, and is applied to the reduced asset value year-on-year. For example, using 30% as the constant:

Raindrop PLC			
Fixed assets			
			Residual value
Vehicles (1999):	Opening value £1,158,000		
Depreciation (Year 1)	£347,400	(30% of £1,158,000)	£810,600
Depreciation (Year 2)	£243,180	(30% of £810,600)	£567,420
Depreciation (Year 3)	£170,226	(30% of £567,420)	£397,194

It is interesting to note the differing asset values obtained using these different methods. For example in Year 1, using the straight line method, the value was £958,000, whereas it was only £810,600 using the reducing balance method. In Year 2, the figure is £758,000 against £567,420, and in Year 3, £558,000 against £397,194.

Regarding depreciation, it must be understood that when an asset is depreciated an annual charge for the use of that asset is made, and that annual charge will appear in the profit & loss account. This charge will therefore show as an expense, and will have the effect of reducing the net profit figure, thus affecting ratios that measure organizational profitability. Similarly, with the depreciation of assets in the balance sheet, all ratios which are based on the asset profile of the organization will also be substantially affected.

The way in which an asset is depreciated is not purely an internal matter for auditors and directors to decide. Guidance is given in SSAPs, and in some countries, there are tax considerations. Some tax relief may be obtained, in the UK for example, in the form of capital allowances; and clearly since depreciation charges affect the profit & loss account, they will also have an effect on the level of taxation.

With the rise of the knowledge-based economy, there are many organizations where intangible assets appear on the balance sheet. Examples of intangible assets are brands, such as the MacDonalds Restaurants 'golden arches', the Lever Brothers 'starburst' and so on. Organizations which invest heavily in intellectual property, such as pharmaceutical companies with research patents, publishers with books, and so on, may also report intangible assets on a balance sheet. These assets are often classed as 'good will' and pose a number of questions. What, for example, is the value of an intangible asset such as a website? The answer is whatever anyone will pay; but this can only be established by selling it! Accountants and auditors frequently have to challenge the basis of valuation and depreciation of such assets. Essentially, similar accounting principles must be applied. But it is very difficult to establish intangible asset values and there are no satisfactory methods that are universally available. Hence this is sometimes used as an 'opportunity' for 'creative accounting'.

What am I bid for the secret to Dr X's Wondercure?

Liabilities

To conclude this overview of the balance sheet it must be remembered that any organization will have liabilities as well as assets. The liabilities of an organization can be:

☞ Current – liabilities that fall due for repayment within one year, such as dividends, taxation, creditors and short-term loans, overdrafts.

☞ Long term – liabilities such as mortgages and debentures, whose repayments are due over a much longer time period.

The financing of an organization as shown on the balance sheet, will comprise:

☞ Share capital which has been issued and paid in full (i.e. what the shareholders have put in).

☞ Any retained earnings (i.e. what the shareholders have not taken out).

CASE STUDY:
RAINDROP PLC (2)

In the example of Raindrop PLC, the organizational accounts show three consecutive years, 1997, 1998 and 1999. The information for public consumption shows that in the three-year period, gross profit has risen from £762,000 to £1,624,000, and net profit from £232,000 to £773,000 (extracted from the trading and profit & loss accounts).

The balance sheets show that over this period the total net assets of Raindrop PLC have increased from £3,946,000 to £6,462,000.

In general it could be said that Raindrop PLC has traded rather well over the period 1997 to 1999, and has husbanded its resources to great effect during that time. However, by conducting financial analysis within the management accounts section, a more informed picture will emerge.

ACTIVITY 3

(1)　From the trading and profit & loss accounts and balance sheets for Raindrop PLC what further information can you derive about the financial performance of the organization?

(2)　If you were an investment adviser, what would be the key points to make to potential investors about the benefits, or otherwise, of investing in Raindrop PLC?

Read on to find out more about how to analyse these accounts.

09-1-4   Management Accounting

Unlike financial accounting, which produces reports primarily aimed at external consumption, management accounting is for internal use only, to assist management in their various planning and decision making processes. Management accounting must be viewed as an essential aspect of the strategic development of the organization, and as such it is a tool to be used in the various processes of the organization and not as an end in itself. Again, unlike financial accounting, which reports on the facts of business transactions, management accounting delves behind the fact and examines the reasons behind the bare bones of transactions involving corporate resources. For example, the sales turnover figures reported in the trading and profit & loss account will show the value of sales over a period of time, but management needs more information concerning, for example:

☞   Which product lines are most successful

☞   Which product/market segments are more responsive to marketing and advertising

☞   Which customers are regular purchasers of the products.

Similarly in the management accountant's examination of the manufacturing accounts of a production organization, various aspects of production control that will impact on the cost of the product need careful examination. Questions arise such as:

☞   How many rejects are there in a production run?
☞   What are the main factors causing rejects to occur?
☞   Can the introduction of a better quality control system lessen the number of rejects?
☞   How much will such a system cost?
☞   Will it be cost-effective?

These questions might be raised from a financial standpoint, but they must be answered for the benefit of the organization.

09-1-5   Ratio Analysis

One of the most important management accounting tools is that of ratio analysis. Ratio analysis seeks to examine the final accounts of the organization by considering these in terms of key ratio groupings. The major groupings for ratio analysis are:

☞ Liquidity

☞ Profitability

☞ Activity

☞ Debt.

Within each of these groupings are ratios that can be used to measure and compare organizational financial performance in order to plan strategically for the future of the organization.

The results of ratio analysis must, however, be considered in the broader context. Several corporate information organizations sell data about companies over the Internet and in hard copy directories that can be quite misleading, as the basic data can be years out of date. With large databases backed by powerful computer systems, they provide management reports and risk/credit ratings which are based solely on ratio analysis of publicly available corporate accounts. This can lead to situations where otherwise respectable organizations can be portrayed as 'corporate disasters', and conversely 'Southsea Bubbles' waiting to burst can be reported as sound investments. It is essential to have the full picture — not just the numbers.

The data for ratio analysis are taken from the final accounts of the organization, the trading and profit & loss accounts and the balance sheet. It could be argued that creative accounting is not illegal and could be portrayed as 'presenting the organization in the best possible light'.

Unethical policies have led in the past to the collapse of organizations, which would be successful under normal market conditions. It is therefore important to ascertain that the financial/accounting standards of an organization are based on an ethical standpoint, which we will consider as a norm:

☞ Integrity

☞ Objectivity

☞ Professionalism

☞ Societal understanding.

Liquidity Ratios

A major aspect of forward planning is the ability of the organization to meet its short-term debts when these become due for payment. In accounting terms, short-term debts are those debts that become due for payment within one year, i.e. from one annual trading period to the next. To meet these short-term debts an organization must have assets that can be made liquid, i.e. easily converted into cash or cash equivalent. In a typical balance sheet, the following assets would be considered as current or easily liquidated in the short term:

- Cash
- Accounts receivable (debtors)
- Bank balances
- Stock (inventory)
- Pre-payments made.

The current liabilities of the organization would include such items as:

- Accounts payable (creditors)
- Notes payable
- Bank credit
- Short-term loans due within a year
- Dividends
- Taxation.

The ideal situation for any organization is that it is sufficiently viable to meet any short-term obligations (current liabilities) from its current asset portfolio.

The three major measures of liquidity are:

(1)   Net Working Capital

(2)   The Current Ratio

(3)   The Acid Test or Quick Ratio.

(1)   Net Working Capital

Net Working Capital (NWC) is calculated by subtracting current liabilities from current assets. As a general rule of thumb, NWC should always be positive, i.e. the organization has more current assets than current liabilities. Situations might arise where the positive difference can be too high, and the organization is not using its current assets efficiently. For example, it might be holding onto too much cash, allowing trade debtors too much time to repay their outstanding bills or having too much money tied up in slow moving stock.

$$Net\ Working\ Capital\ =\ Current\ Assets\ -\ Current\ Liabilities$$

If we examine the situation concerning Raindrop PLC (see previous data) the following information concerning liquidity is shown.

1997 Net Working Capital   =   £1,534,000 – £510,000   = £1,024,000

1998 Net Working Capital   =   £1,941,000 – £683,000   = £1,258,000

1999 Net Working Capital   =   £2,585,000 – £1,168,000 = £1,417,000

From these calculations Raindrop PLC appears to be able to meet any short-term debts from their short-term assets with ease.

(2)   The Current Ratio

This is calculated as:

$$Current\ Ratio\ =\ \frac{Current\ Assets}{Current\ Liabilities}$$

The situation for Raindrop PLC over the three-year period 1997 – 1999 appears as follows:

$$1997\ Current\ Ratio\ =\ \frac{£1,534,000}{£510,000}\ =\ 3{:}1$$

$$1998\ Current\ Ratio\ =\ \frac{£1,941,000}{£683,000}\ =\ 2.84{:}1$$

$$1999\ Current\ Ratio\ =\ \frac{£2,585,000}{£1,168,000}\ =\ 2.2{:}1$$

In general, an efficient current ratio should be approximately between 1.5:1 and 2:1. This guideline is not carved in stone and is dependent upon the accepted sector norm. Supermarkets work on a ratio of approximately 0.6:1 and are certainly viable. These ratios don't really work for businesses with mainly cash sales. However, from the calculations, it would appear that Raindrop were seen to be more liquid in 1997 than they needed to be and have made moves to rectify this situation, so that by 1999 their current ratio is getting closer to an acceptable level.

(3) The Acid Test (Quick Ratio)

It is generally considered that the least liquid of an organization's current assets is its stock holding or inventory figures. Most financial management analysts consider that a better barometer of an organization's liquidity is the Acid Test Ratio, which removes the least liquid of the firm's assets from the liquidity ratio measurement.

$$Acid\ Test\ Ratio\ =\ \frac{Current\ Assets - Stock}{Current\ Liabilities}$$

The situation at Raindrop PLC. for the period 1997 – 1999 is as follows:

$$1997\ Acid\ Test\ Ratio\ =\ \frac{£1,534,000 - £682,000}{£510,000}\ =\ \frac{£852,000}{£510,000}\ =\ 1.7:1$$

$$1998\ Acid\ Test\ Ratio\ =\ \frac{£1,941,000 - £792,000}{£683,000}\ =\ \frac{£1,149,000}{£683,000}\ =\ 1.7:1$$

$$1999\ Acid\ Test\ Ratio\ =\ \frac{£2,585,000 - £925,000}{£1,168,000}\ =\ \frac{£1,660,000}{£1,168,000}\ =\ 1.4:1$$

Again as a general guideline, the Acid Test Ratio should appear within a range of 0.8:1 and 1:1, and many organizations see the ideal as a 1:1 ratio. This is where the current liabilities can be met by all current assets except for the stock holding or inventory figure.

To summarize the liquidity situation at Raindrop, it would appear that they are too liquid and have adopted a rather safe and conservative stance with regard to liquidity. However, if the year 2000 reflects the downward shift in liquidity holding, this would be to the good of the organization.

The ability of an organization to meet its short-term debt impacts on the ability of the organization to buy goods on credit. The ability to borrow short-term and long-term money depends on the organization's performance in this respect.

Profitability Ratios

When asked 'What is the main objective of the organization?' many people reply 'To make a profit'. However this is not always true and a better way of considering profit is as a measure of the success of the strategic policies adopted by an organization. There are many different ways in which profit can be measured by corporate management, but the two main categories of measuring profitability are:

☞ Profits measured against sales
☞ Profits measured against assets.

Continuing with the example of Raindrop, the profitability ratios that will be computed are:

☞ Gross Profit Margin
☞ Net Profit Margin
☞ Return on Assets.

(1)   Gross Profit Margin (GP)

The Gross Profit Margin (GP) measures the difference between the sales turnover achieved by an organization and the direct costs involved in producing these sales. The computation to find the GP % is as follows:

$$\textit{Gross Profit Margin}\,\% \;=\; \frac{\textit{Gross Profit}}{\textit{Sales}} \;\times\; \frac{100}{1}$$

With Raindrop PLC the following GP margins % were achieved during the 1997 – 1999 period:

$$1997\ \textit{Gross Profit}\,\% \;=\; \frac{£762,000}{£2,624,000} \;\times\; \frac{100}{1} \;=\; 29\%$$

$$1998\ \textit{Gross Profit}\,\% \;=\; \frac{£975,000}{£2,899,000} \;\times\; \frac{100}{1} \;=\; 33.6\%$$

www.universal-manager.co.uk

$$1999 \ Gross \ Profit\% \ = \ \frac{£1,624,000}{£3,666,000} \ x \ \frac{100}{1} \ = \ 44.3\%$$

From these calculations it can be seen that the GP achieved during this three-year period has risen considerably from 1997 to 1999. The reasons for this increase will be due in no small measure to particular policies adopted by the corporate management from close analysis of previous financial and management data. Specific reasons could include:

☞ Pricing policy reflecting demand

☞ Marketing/Advertising strategies

☞ Lower production costs.

(2) Net Profit Margin

The 'true' net profit will be the final profit made after all costs and expenses have been taken from the sales income. In some organizations, net profit may be the term used to indicate 'operating profit', which is the situation with Raindrop. Many net profit calculations will be computed prior to considering any interest expense and/or any taxation expense, and these may be shown as EBIT (Earnings Before Interest and Tax). It is a 'must' for managers to be sure what net profit actually refers to, as there is no clear and accepted convention for the various profit terminologies.

In the example of Raindrop, the net profit is really the operating profit as it excludes both interest and taxation expenses. The net profit margin is calculated as follows:

$$Net \ Profit\% \ = \ \frac{Net \ Profit}{Sales} \ x \ \frac{100}{1}$$

For Raindrop the 1997 – 1999 situation is:

$$1997 \ Net \ Profit\% \ = \ \frac{£232,000}{£2,624,000} \ x \ \frac{100}{1} \ = \ 8.84\%$$

$$1998 \ Net \ Profit\% \ = \ \frac{£430,000}{£2,899,000} \ x \ \frac{100}{1} \ = \ 14.83\%$$

$$1999 \ Net \ Profit\% \ = \ \frac{£773,000}{£3,666,000} \ x \ \frac{100}{1} \ = \ 21.09\%$$

Financial Performance

The most interesting aspect of the net profit calculations is that the results mirror the increases in gross profit during the three-year period, increasing from just under 9% in 1997 to just over 21% in 1999. These net profit (operating profit) figures, which are calculated before interest and taxation expenses, indicate that sales turnover has increased dramatically in 1999. At the same time, operating costs have been kept substantially in check, and the increased advertising expenditure between 1998 and 1999 is apparently resulting in increased sales.

(3) Return on Assets (ROA)

The profitability measures computed above have measured profits made by the organization in terms of income generated through sales of the product or service. Another way of considering profit is by measuring the efficiency of asset utilization in generating profit. The computation used to calculate Return on Assets is:

$$ROA = \frac{Net\ Profit}{Total\ Assets} \times \frac{100}{1}$$

Continuing with Raindrop, the ROA situation appears as follows:

$$1997\ ROA = \frac{£232,000}{£4,856,000} \times \frac{100}{1} = 4.8\%$$

$$1998\ ROA = \frac{£430,000}{£5,955,000} \times \frac{100}{1} = 7.2\%$$

$$1999\ ROA = \frac{£773,000}{£8,030,000} \times \frac{100}{1} = 9.6\%$$

The percentage profit made through asset utilization is lower than the ratio of profitability to sales, but the interesting aspect of this calculation is that again an upward movement is apparent. The Return on Assets has increased over the three-year period from 4.8% in 1997 to 9.6% in 1999.

By comparing the net profit margin with the return on assets calculation, we can deduce what type of market Raindrop operates in. As Raindrop appears not to be in an extreme situation, it can be assumed that they are involved in a medium activity market place — possibly a small manufacturing enterprise, or possibly a fashion retailer.

For example, two diverse types of market which will, by their nature, have distinct pricing and asset management characteristics are the motor vehicle manufacturing market and the retail grocery market. In the motor vehicle market, there is a need for substantial asset investment to pay for high research and development costs and to set up an effective production line. Consequently the end product is one of high unit cost aligned with infrequent purchases. In the retail grocery market, there is little asset expenditure on costly areas such as research and development. However, the high street or shopping centre competition between leading retailers is primarily price based, resulting in low profit margins and high stockturn rates.

Profitability is not to be taken in isolation as an end in itself. Organizations will have continuity and growth as long-term goals. Profit is however an efficient indicator of how well current pricing, marketing, and product/services policies are working — it is a measure of successful strategic policy.

Activity Ratios

In this part of ratio analysis, the emphasis of the management information relates to the way in which the various financial assets of the organization are being managed and utilized. These ratios are often referred to as Efficiency Ratios as they answer the question often posed by the owners of the organization: 'Is management controlling our assets effectively and efficiently?'.

The main ratios to be considered in this category are:

(1)   Stock (Inventory) Turnover Rate

(2)   Average Debt Collection Period (Debtor Days)

(3)   Total Asset Turnover.

(1)   Stock Turnover Rate

The purpose here is to show how often the average stockholding of the organization is 'turned over' or sold during the year. In general, the more often the stock is turned over, the better for the organization, as this will show that the stock holding of the organization is a liquid resource and is not sitting on shelves as a depreciating or redundant resource.

Financial Performance

As with other examples, the stock turnover rate is affected by the area of industry that the organization is in. For example, a bakery will have a much higher stock turnover rate than a manufacturer of fireworks. It is necessary to look at previous results over time and also to draw comparisons between the organization and industry sector averages.

Many accountants will use the formula:

$$Stockturn = \frac{Sales}{Average\ Stock}$$

to calculate stock turnover rate, which is perfectly acceptable and helpful in measuring efficiency. However a formula which gives a cleaner and clearer interpretation is one which replaces sales by cost of sales, thus removing any imbalances from the calculation caused by changing profit markups which may be included in the sales figure. So we have:

$$Stockturn = \frac{Cost\ of\ Sales}{Average\ Stock}$$

For Raindrop:

$$1997\ Stockturn = \frac{£1,862,000}{£682,000} = 2.7\ times$$

$$1998\ Stockturn = \frac{£1,924,000}{£792,000} = 2.4\ times$$

$$1999\ Stockturn = \frac{£2,042,000}{£925,000} = 2.2\ times$$

Raindrop should be aware of a reducing trend with regard to their stock turnover rate, bearing in mind that the guideline for stock turnover is the higher the better. An investigation should be undertaken by management in order to understand the causes of, or contributing factors to, change in this activity/efficiency ratio. Possible causes could be:

☞ Increased costs of goods, or
☞ A decision to hold larger stocks for economies of scale, or
☞ Simply demand is falling — leaving the organization with more stock on the shelves, or
☞ Inefficient management of supply.

(2) Average Debt Collection Period

All organizations will have some form of credit policy — a policy that determines the time allowed for its customers to pay for goods and/or services. Very few firms operate today on a cash only policy (with the notable exception of many retailers, particularly supermarkets), and it is of therefore utmost importance that where credit is given, credit control procedures are in place. Many organizations will develop a credit control policy in theory but will fail to implement it in practice, which can prove to be very costly for them in the long term. The debtors of an organization can cause cash flow problems by not heeding the credit terms stipulated. In 1997 the UK Government intervened to introduce laws to penalize firms who seriously disregarded the credit terms of suppliers. It was found that the size of the firm played an important role on the ethical stance taken with regard to paying outstanding debts. The larger the organization, the more likely it was to hold off its payments in order to achieve financial benefit through an unfair extension of credit periods.

Consider for example, an organization that calculates its financial well-being on a credit policy of 30 days' credit. Any drift upward from 30 days will be an on-cost to the organization and could adversely affect its profitability.

The formula to calculate the average debtor collection period is as follows:

$$Debtor\ Days\ =\ \frac{Debtors}{Average\ Sales\ per\ Day}$$

where: $$Average\ Sales\ per\ Day\ =\ \frac{Sales}{365}$$

For Raindrop the situation is as follows:

$$1997\ Debtor\ Days\ =\ \frac{£520,000}{£2,624,000}\ \times\ \frac{365}{1}\ =\ 72.3\ days$$

$$1998\ Debtor\ Days\ =\ \frac{£683,000}{£2,899,000}\ \times\ \frac{365}{1}\ =\ 86\ days$$

$$1999\ Debtor\ Days\ =\ \frac{£892,000}{£3,666,000}\ \times\ \frac{365}{1}\ =\ 88.8\ days$$

So far in our analysis of the financial performance of Raindrop, nothing has shown as much of a financial control problem as these figures. What is clear is that there is no control in place with regard to outstanding debtors and that the situation has become decidedly worse in the period 1997 – 1999, during which debt collection has gone from 72 days to almost 90 days.

This kind of problem would be an issue of immediate concern to the financial well-being of any organization. What we had earlier thought of as improving trends at Raindrop, we should now question in light of this poor performance indicator.

(3) Total Asset Turnover

This ratio shows the relationship between investment in assets and the corresponding sales achieved by the organization through its investment policy. As with many previous ratios, care must be taken in the interpretation of this ratio. The type of industry, product, market, and lease or buy decisions will all affect total asset turnover. For example, an organization involved in market research will have a different asset profile from a motor manufacturer. As the market researchers need fewer assets, their total asset turnover ratio will be much higher than that of the motor manufacturer. It is therefore imperative that like for like comparisons are drawn, either with past performance within the organization, or against similar organizations.

The computation is as follows:

$$\text{Total Asset Turnover} = \frac{\text{Sales}}{\text{Total Assets}}$$

For Raindrop:

$$1997 \text{ Total Asset Turnover} = \frac{£2,624,000}{£4,856,000} = 0.54 \text{ times}$$

$$1998 \text{ Total Asset Turnover} = \frac{£2,899,000}{£5,955,000} = 0.49 \text{ times}$$

$$1999 \text{ Total Asset Turnover} = \frac{£3,666,000}{£8,030,000} = 0.46 \text{ times}$$

Again the rule is the higher the better. The total asset turnover performance of Raindrop over the past three years should cause the directors some concern as there has been a steady decline in this ratio.

In most medium to large business organizations ownership and control are quite separate and different aspects. Activity/Efficiency ratios indicate to the owners (shareholders) of the organization how well their salaried managers are utilizing their assets.

44

Debt Ratios

These ratios are often referred to as calculations of the leverage or gearing of an organization.

In any organization there are both short- and long-term liabilities. As previously discussed, the difference between short-term assets and liabilities will indicate the ability or otherwise of an organization to meet its short-term debts, and this confirms the liquidity of the organization. The ability of an organization to meet its short-term debt will also play an important part in determining its long-term funding strategy.

Where long-term loans exist, the organization must have sufficient funds from which to pay any interest charges accrued against the loans, and this is why most profit & loss accounts will show profit as EBIT (earnings before interest and tax). In the example that has been used as an illustration, no interest on borrowing is shown. However the ratio that would be used is as follows:

$$Interest\ Cover\ =\ \frac{Operating\ Profit}{Interest\ Charges}$$

This ratio is also referred to as the TIE Ratio (Times Interest Earned).

Essentially there are two ratios that are of value in assessing the debt burden of an organization, these being:

☞ The Debt Ratio
☞ The Debt/Equity Ratio.

The Debt Ratio gives a clear picture of what proportion of the assets of an organization are financed by liabilities (as opposed to financed by assets) and is calculated as follows:

$$Debt\ Ratio\ \%\ =\ \frac{Total\ Liabilities}{Total\ Assets}\ x\ \frac{100}{1}$$

The Debt/Equity Ratio compares long-term liabilities with the finance provided by the owners in terms of shareholding (equity). This measure is calculated as follows:

$$Debt/Equity\ Ratio\ \%\ =\ \frac{Long\text{-}term\ Liabilities}{Shareholders'\ Equity}\ x\ \frac{100}{1}$$

Financial Performance

To return to Raindrop, the following computations show the debt burden carried during the period 1997 – 1999:

$$\textit{1997 Debt Ratio \%} = \frac{£910,000}{£4,856,000} \times \frac{100}{1} = 18.74\%$$

$$\textit{1998 Debt Ratio \%} = \frac{£1,083,000}{£5,955,000} \times \frac{100}{1} = 18.19\%$$

$$\textit{1999 Debt Ratio \%} = \frac{£1,568,000}{£8,030,000} \times \frac{100}{1} = 19.53\%$$

Raindrop appears to be in a most comfortable position in respect to total assets to total liabilities, with less than 20% of their asset base taken up by liabilities.

$$\textit{1997 Debt/Equity Ratio \%} = \frac{£400,000}{£3,000,000} \times \frac{100}{1} = 13.33\%$$

$$\textit{1998 Debt/Equity Ratio \%} = \frac{£400,000}{£3,600,000} \times \frac{100}{1} = 11.11\%$$

$$\textit{1999 Debt/Equity Ratio \%} = \frac{£400,000}{£4,800,000} \times \frac{100}{1} = 8.33\%$$

It appears that Raindrop have made a conscious decision not to incur any long-term borrowing and have stayed with their only commitment of £400,000 in the form of prior charge capital as debentures. On this profile, the organization has decided to fund the future through an extension of share ownership rather than borrow externally from banks or other sources of long-term borrowing.

From the above computations, it is clear that Raindrop wish to keep debt to a minimum in the short term. Indeed over the three year period 1997 – 1999 Raindrop has increased its share options and at the same time they have reduced borrowing in real terms from 13% to just over 8%.

The gearing of an organization will have an impact on how likely it is that it will be able to secure future long-term borrowing from external sources. If there is a high debt ratio, the likelihood of future substantial external borrowing is reduced, because the quality of security available is diluted.

www.universal-manager.co.uk

ACTIVITY 4

(1)   From your own organization obtain a copy of the last Annual Report, and examine the Chairman's statement for past performance and future intent. What does he/she say?

(2)   Now look at the published accounts summaries and attempt to calculate some of the ratios indicated in this section. Do the results support the statement of future intent?

Now read on.

09-2 FORECASTING TECHNIQUES

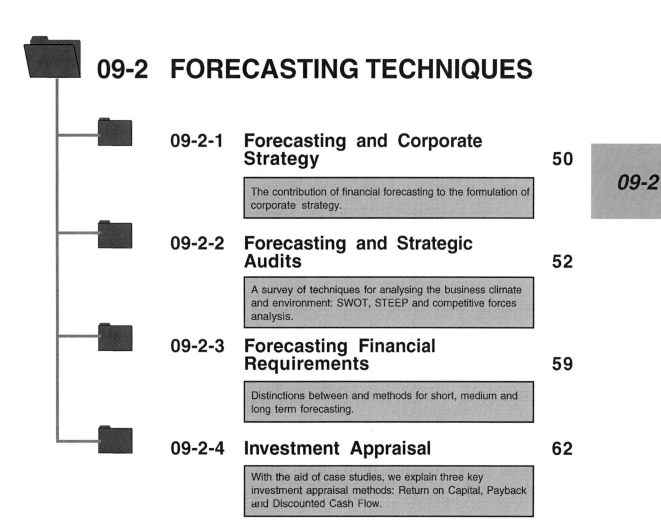

09-2

09-2 FORECASTING TECHNIQUES

'Don't never prophesy — onless ye know.'
(James Russell Lowell 1819 – 1891)

Financial forecasting relies heavily on the processes used by an organization for budgeting. However, it is important that managers do not immerse themselves in budgetary detail to the exclusion of the 'big picture'. In other words, financial forecasting must take account of the organization's strategic objectives and the environment within which it operates.

Another important facet of financial forecasting is the analysis of past performance. An organization's past performance gives the best data on the ingredients of success (or failure) given particular sets of circumstances. However, unquestioning extrapolation of past results to derive a forecast will be extremely misleading (although the figures might look good on paper); even careful trend extrapolation alone is unlikely to produce a good financial forecast.

Trend extrapolation is a term used in statistics which means that a series of past performances are recorded and a trend line is fitted for the period observed. To predict future occurrences, this trend is extended or projected into the future to give a forecast of future performance. A major problem with this type of forecasting is that the main assumption is based on future conditions being the same as the past, which certainly is not always the case.

09-2-1 Forecasting and Corporate Strategy

The corporate strategy is the starting point on which to base plans for the development of the business organization. Corporate strategy is the overarching plan of the organization which will detail the way in which it will seek to accomplish the goals and objectives set by corporate management on behalf of the stakeholders. From a financial perspective, corporate strategic management is all about the allocation and utilization of corporate resources to ensure efficiency and effectiveness in the pursuit of corporate objectives.

A key starting point for any organization embarking on a strategic management process is to articulate clearly the mission of the organization. This is a clear statement outlining the business that the organization is in, encompassing:

☞ The nature and purpose of the organization

☞ The desired position within its markets that the organization wishes to achieve

☞ The organization's key values and priorities

☞ The future wishes and hopes of the organization

☞ The main customer/user groups that the organization wishes to serve.

From the mission statement will flow the clear and unambiguous objectives that the organization wishes to pursue, objectives based on:

☞ Economy, i.e. the way in which organizational resources are utilized in pursuit of organizational objectives, and the way in which costs are controlled, standards maintained and budgets applied.

☞ Efficiency, i.e. the way in which productivity can be developed by correct financial measures in relation to organizational inputs and outputs.

☞ Effectiveness, i.e. the way in which desired objectives become realizable outcomes through correct analysis of the organization's internal and external environments, and through successful targeting of products/ services to the appropriate market segment(s).

It is also essential that any organization establishes systems which will monitor and measure performance, to ensure that objectives are achieved and budgets are followed. Therefore organizations need to be able to translate objectives into quantifiable concepts, particularly profit targets.

There are many sources of information and expertise on the methodologies of defining mission statements and communicating them within organizations, and it is not our purpose to examine the subject here. Suffice to say that communication of the mission statement to all stakeholders is fundamental, and that attempting to develop forecasts and budgets in isolation from the corporate mission and objectives will inevitably lead to incorrect assumptions and misleading financial models.

ACTIVITY 5

(1)　Does your organization have a mission statement? If not, what do you think it should be?

(2)　If it does have a mission statement, is there a formal process for ensuring that stakeholders are involved in its formulation and communication, such as Investors in People?

Now read on.

09-2-2　Forecasting and Strategic Audits

As part of the formulation of corporate strategy, prior to any forecasting, organizations must conduct a series of audits in order to establish the assumptions on which objectives (financial or otherwise) will be based.

A SWOT audit is usual for taking an internal view of:

　Strengths
　Weaknesses
　Opportunities
　Threats.

By auditing the SWOT profile of the organization, especially in financial and resource terms, it is possible to identify the main issues that will inform assumptions made in financial forecasting.

ACTIVITY 6
GALASHIELDS GORILLAS (1)

09-2

The fictional Galashields Gorillas ice hockey team has been promoted this season into ice hockey's Premier Division. One problem that faces it, however, is that its stadium is not up to the required standards for spectator safety and quality of the ice surface.

The total cost of refurbishment is quoted to be £1M, a substantial sum of money and one which the club cannot meet on its own. The local authority is aware of the sporting interest generated by a premiership ice hockey team in the locality and has promised to cover half the costs in one lump sum.

The following financial data is available for the six-month period January to June 2000:

(a)   The club will have to pay the contractor as follows:
      £500,000 on 1 January, £250,000 on 1 March and £250,000 on 1 May.

(b)   Galashields Borough Council will pay Galashields Gorillas £500,000 on 1 March.

(c)   A player will be sold in January for £70,000, another in February for £65,000, and finally one more in June for £48,000.

(d)   Expenses on match days allocated to each month are shown in the following table, together with the anticipated receipts from matches played.

	January	February	March	April	May	June
Expenses	£16,500	£14,000	£17,500	£16,500	£13,600	£15,000
Receipts	£58,600	£52,200	£63,500	£56,000	£51,500	£61,400

(e)   Fixed expenses for the club are £4,500 per month.

(f)   Variable expenses are half of the home game receipts and are settled one month in arrears.

(g)   The receipts from home games in December 1999 were £64,000.

(h)   The cash balance in the bank on 1 January 2000 is £134,600.

Financial Performance

Consider the situation facing the Galashields Gorillas Ice Hockey team. Carry out a brief SWOT analysis that might be appropriate to the future financial forecasts for the club.

You should consider the pros and cons of Premiership status in terms of the impact on business through potentially increased revenues, higher media profile, etc. How are improvements going to be financed? What are the implications of the answers to this question in terms of strengths, weaknesses, opportunities and threats? What opportunities and threats accompany the promotion to the Premier Division? Consider the longer term as well as the short-term. Will the team survive in the Premiership in business terms? Will they be relegated next season? What might be the implications of this?

Refer to Appendix 1 for a commentary.

If the SWOT analysis (Appendix 1) is considered in conjunction with a cash budget computation (see page 89), the Galashields Gorillas Ice Hockey Club would have a much clearer picture with which to determine their future direction. For example, many of the financial calculations may have been made on figures available from past records, and these are records of a team which is not yet in the Premiership!

To all intents and purposes, the budget preparation process is a tool of organizational forecasting which plays an important role in determining the ability of the organization to follow a particular future path and achieve its corporate strategic objectives.

The opportunities for a greater income base through avenues such as sponsorship, increased merchandising revenue, increased turnstile prices and larger crowds may not have been part of the original computation.

For the external environment which will influence the forecast direction of the organization a PEST/STEP analysis is used:

- ☞ Social
- ☞ Technological
- ☞ Economic
- ☞ Political.

STEP is sometimes extended to STEEP or even STEEPL, the other external environments being:

- ☞ (physical) Environment
- ☞ Legal.

These are sometimes analysed separately depending on the nature of the organization. Examples of each of the environmental factors are given in the Personal Development Planning Toolkit, available at:

www.universal-manager.co.uk

 ACTIVITY 7

With respect to your own organization, list the three most significant external environmental influences that may affect your organization's direction in each of the four STEP categories.

Now read on.

SWOT and STEEPL analyses are useful exercises in identifying issues, but they are of limited use. They do not suggest a framework for further analysis or action; and importantly, they do not help us understand how identified issues interact or are co-dependent. Professor M.E. Porter of Harvard Business School provides us with a framework which is of far greater use for financial management in the context of a modern, competitive environment.

His model identifies 'five competitive forces that determine industry profitability', and these are illustrated as follows:

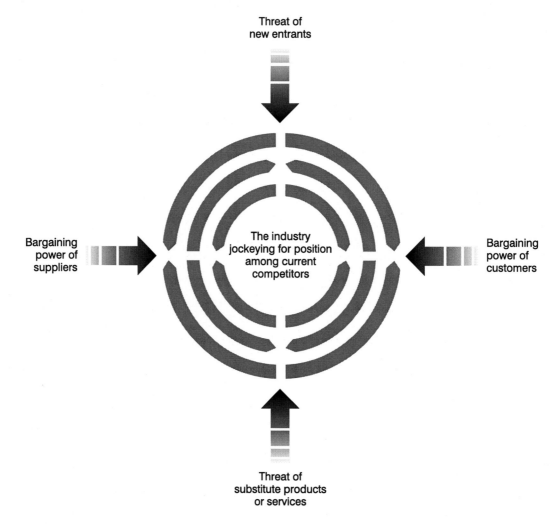

(Source: M E Porter (1979), 'Competition Shapes Strategy', *Harvard Business Review*, March–April.)

These forces apply in any industry, whether it is product or service oriented, and in many circumstances will also apply to not-for-profit organizations. The five forces are the main influences on return on investment, whose constituent parts are price, cost and investment required. If an organization is striving to maximize return on investment in a particular industry sector, then from a financial management point of view these five forces embrace and relate the most important issues which we might express through SWOT or STEEPL analyses.

The usefulness of Porter's model arises partly from the detail in which the five forces are analysed further, enabling the managers to formulate strategy and take decisions about appropriate tactics. The most important elements of the five forces are illustrated by Porter as follows:

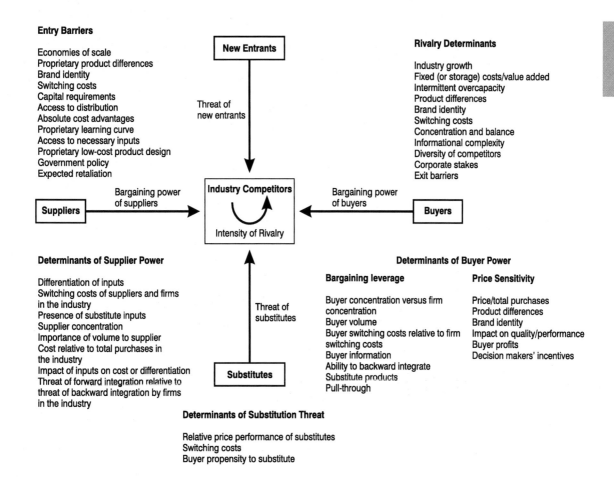

(Source: M E Porter (1985), *Competitive Advantage*, Free Press.)

One important aspect of Porter's model is that it shows us how these competitive elements might interact. Frequently, organizations make strategic moves for short-term gain without fully appreciating how their moves will prompt competitor response in the medium to long term. It is, however, important to appreciate that the model is not rigid for any particular industry — it is dynamic with some firms being able to change industry structure (for better or for worse).

Porter's model also shows how financial management is integrated into every aspect of competitive analysis. This is not necessarily the case with the less detailed SWOT and STEP approach.

CASE STUDY: AMSTRAD

In the 1980s, PC manufacturers such as IBM were pursuing a strategy of high price maintenance, potentially allowing room for a low cost operator to enter the market. Amstrad had worked out a way of introducing low cost, cheap personal computers and peripherals into the market. They established a new brand identity underpinned by absolute cost advantages. Amstrad PCs were typically manufactured in very short runs using 'old technology' components — no longer used by their competitors and sourced globally. Interestingly, although Alan Sugar (Amstrad's CEO) stated that he was going for 'big blue', his first target market segment was not IBM PC users but the typewriter user. In other words, Amstrad grew the low-cost end of the personal computer market during the 1980s by attracting first-time buyers of PCs. By the 1990s, not only had the established computer manufacturers responded with their own low-cost models, but Amstrad had shown other 'manufacturers' the way to overcome entry barriers to the industry. Many new entrants set up build-to-order operations using a variety of component technologies. In addition, existing industry manufacturers ensured that their marketing initiatives encouraged the buyer to take an interest in what was inside the PC ('Intel inside', etc.) making it harder for old technology to be exploited in this way again. (Microsoft's emergence at the same time as the globally dominant provider of operating systems and proprietary applications software outdated Amstrad's technology rapidly.) Amstrad's intervention helped to exploit changes in the industry structure — breaking down barriers to entry, altering the mix of supplier power determinants and changing the balance within the determinants of buyer power. Amstrad's short-term gain led to industry responses that closed off the opportunity which Amstrad had exploited. Both IBM and Amstrad re-invented themselves. Neither remained a leader in the PC market.

PAUSE TO REFLECT

Consider Porter's elements of industry structure in relation to your own organization. Overall, which of the five competitive forces most influences your organization currently? Do you anticipate that the balance of competitive forces might change for your organization during the next 1 – 3 years? What impact will this have on your job?

09-2-3 Forecasting Financial Requirements

If we again consider the financial forecast for Galashields Gorillas, the following matters are extremely pressing:

☞ The acquisition of operating capital to meet the requirement of a new stadium, with sufficient capital to meet the forecast expense categories for the ensuing season/financial period.

☞ The development of a sales forecast to cover the same period, to take into account the increased revenue opportunities which accompany Premiership status, such as increased pricing policies, television rights, merchandising opportunities, etc.

☞ The preparation of forecast budgets to cover all the key areas of forecast income and expenditure, such as player sales/purchases, receipts, running costs for utilities, etc.

☞ Evaluating the net worth of the Galashields Gorillas as a corporate entity, and considering 'what if forecasts', e.g. a share issue as opposed to borrowing for a forecasted asset requirement.

In fact, the Gorillas' financial accountant needs to prepare (or revisit) the four main financial forecasts which any organization requires:

☞ Sales or revenue forecast (which is translated into sales targets)
☞ Cost and overhead forecast (which is translated into cost budgets)
☞ Capital expenditure forecast (which is translated into the capital expenditure budget)
☞ Cash forecast.

In addition, forecasts of the profit & loss account and balance sheet may be prepared together with forecasts of key ratios. These forecasts are particularly useful if external financing of, say, the capital budget is required. They will become essential ingredients of the business plan for the external financier.

Forecast Categories

The simplest way of categorizing forecasts is by time as follows:

(1) Short-term forecasts
(2) Medium-term forecasts
(3) Long-term forecasts.

(1)   Short-term forecasts

These will tend to be no more than a year, or a season in the case of Galashields, or a financial period as in the case of Renowindo Ltd (see Case Studies in Sections 09-2-4, 09-4-2 and 09-4-5).

The data from which to forecast financial projections will be found from:

☛   The immediate past trading and financial results available
☛   A check on current activities
☛   Any variances from current plans
☛   An audit of the internal strengths and weaknesses.

(2)   Medium-term forecasts

The time span for this category is generally considered to be up to three years — basically a planning and forecasting buffer between short-term and long-term forecasts. The major benefit to an organization of medium-term forecasts is to enable management to fully analyse strategic policies to provide short-term success, and finely tune and develop plans from these.

(3)   Long-term forecasts

The time span for long-term forecasts is over 3 years — usually 3 – 5 years. However, there is a growing trend to shorten the time span for these forecasts. This reflects the increasingly rapid pace of change impinging on all walks of life, primarily due to information communication technology. ICT has 'shrunk the world' with the result that:

☛   Global trading in stocks and shares is continuous and becoming more individualized rather than institutionalized (through personal share dealing on dot-com sites for example).

☛   Money markets move very rapidly, meaning that political changes can occur overnight, exchange rates change in seconds, and so on.

☛   Stakeholder confidence can be built and lost very rapidly through the availability of communications media.

☛   Geographically remote values and events can have an impact at home where previously they were of no local significance.

Long-term forecasts are in some ways the most difficult to define. It is essential in long-term forecasting to give detailed consideration to the macro environment within which the organization operates. This is where two of the three models already discussed come into play:

☞ STEEPL identifies the macro environmental issues which are affecting and will affect the organization

☞ Porter's models help to translate the macro issues into detailed decisions and actions — formulating the strategy and articulating the tactics.

SWOT (not particularly useful for long-term planning) identifies the 'here and now' issues and immediate short/medium term influences.

 ACTIVITY 8

Consider the markets for personal computers and mobile phones over the last five years.

(1) List the various areas of change that have occurred such as price, availability and size.

(2) Now consider the impact of these changes on the manufacturing organizations within their various product/markets in terms of marketing, distribution, and financial forecasting.

(3) What might the impact be on these organizations as the technologies merge?

(4)   Finally, consider the way in which change has manifested itself within your own product or service market, and examine the way in which your organization forecasts for future change and its impact on financial control measures.

Refer to Appendix 1 for a commentary before continuing.

 ## 09-2-4   Investment Appraisal

The success derived from following a particular strategic direction will rely extensively on the probity of an organization's financial management, especially in the way in which investment decisions are made.

Organizations should invest in capital and other projects that will ensure the future health of the organization, by allowing the management to:

☞   Improve the effectiveness and efficiency of production methods

☞   Invest in new technology

☞   Research and develop new products and/or applications

☞   Develop new methods of marketing, e.g. via the Internet

☞   Enter previously inaccessible product areas/markets (by direct entry, partnerships or acquisitions for example).

Forecasting future financial returns is more commonly referred to as 'Investment Appraisal', and is based upon the requirement to reach the financial decision that by investing in a project, an organization will find itself in a better position than it is currently.

As previously mentioned, any financial decision about the future must be completely compatible with the strategic objectives of the organization, especially in relation to whether the organization is a 'profit maximizer' or a 'profit optimizer'. Computations must show that the forecast returns meet a predetermined and required rate of return.

www.universal-manager.co.uk

The decision to invest in future projects is part of the skill of project planning, and it is an important facet in developing the long-term strategic aims and objectives of the organization. It is important that managers adopt a framework to investigate and analyse potential financial investment opportunities, including methods to assess the financial returns to be achieved from any such opportunity.

Investment Appraisal Checklist

09-2

☞ Consider potential investment opportunities in line with the intended corporate strategy of the organization.

☞ Conduct an initial shortlisting of opportunities to eliminate those which are not fully consistent with planned strategic objectives.

☞ Apply operational performance measures to prioritize potential investment opportunities. These will include quantitative and qualitative measures. Project managers will frequently employ sophisticated methods to make a quantitative assessment of risk, for example.

☞ Decide on which projects are most suitable to pursue in relation to the financial aims of the organization.

Managers' unwillingness to allocate resources to investment opportunities was summarized in *Capital Budgeting for the 1990s* by R.H. Pike (1988, Chartered Institute of Management Accountants) as follows:

☞ Lack of profit opportunity
☞ Economic uncertainty
☞ Unwillingness to increase levels of borrowing
☞ Lack of available capital
☞ Lack of skilled managers to implement investment opportunities.

Selecting the right investment appraisal technique is essential to ensure that decisions are made objectively. The main techniques are discussed on the following pages.

The basis of project planning and investment appraisal should include the following points:

☞ *A clear definition of the strategic objectives of the organization.*

☞ *Analysis and identification of those projects that will lead to fulfilling organizational objectives.*

☞ *Consideration of the costs and benefits associated with each potential project.*

Forecasting Returns On Investment (ROI)

There are three commonly used methods for the investment evaluation of financial projects, these being:

(1) Return on Capital Invested

(2) The Payback Period

(3) Discounted Cash Flow.

Each method has its uses, but each has some disadvantages.

(1) Return on Capital Invested (RCI)

An advantage of this method is that it is simple to calculate in terms of the time taken and the computation itself. RCI is built around the concept of profit and it considers all profits generated by projects over their forecast life. It concentrates on earnings/profit rather than cash flow and is therefore of more interest to 'outsiders' than management.

This method does have the disadvantages that it does not:

☞ Give consideration to the present value of money
☞ Consider the timing of the return on investment
☞ Give weightings to the duration of the earnings.

CASE STUDY:
RENOWINDO LTD (1)

09-2

Renowindo is a recent entrant into the double glazing market. It makes windows and doors at a small manufacturing base on the outskirts of Gravesend in the South East of England, and sells its products direct to consumers.

Renowindo Ltd is faced with deciding which is the better of two investment opportunities, both costing the same amount of capital (£50,000) and both forecasting the same return over a five year period (£75,000).

However, as can be seen from the following, the earnings profile with respect to time for each project is completely different.

Project	2001	2002	2003	2004	2005
A	£5,000	£10,000	£15,000	£20,000	£25,000
B	£25,000	£18,500	£16,500	£10,000	£5,000

As can be seen by using the RCI method, Renowindo would have to consider both projects as equally acceptable. However project B should be the preferred option as it returns the capital sum more quickly thus releasing funds for reinvestment.

CASE STUDY:
BUNTY'S BOXES (1)

A small organization, Bunty's Boxes, manufactures presentation and gift boxes for the wristwatch market and has been in business for only five years. During this time, sales have improved year-on-year and the directors of the organization are now discussing the budget plans for Bunty's Boxes for the coming year.

Using the same methodology, the forecast shows the following:

Project	Total Earnings	Capital Investment	Net Earnings	Project Life	Average
Y	£50,000	£40,000	£10,000	1 year	£10,000
Z	£140,000	£40,000	£100,000	10 years	£10,000

The annual average earnings from both projects are equal, and therefore either could be chosen as the duration of the project is not considered in this method, just the annual average.

The obvious problem in using this method of analysis is that the duration of the earnings is not considered. In this example, one project over time returns 10 times more than the other for the same capital investment.

(2) Payback Period

The key criterion for success using this forecasting tool for financial investment is the speed at which the initial financial outlay is recouped by the organization.

As with ROI, payback period fails to consider the time value of money. Other disadvantages of this method are:

☛ The total life of the project is not taken into consideration.

☛ It does not have the ability to distinguish between projects that may have the same payback period of time.

☛ The profit profile over the total life of the project is not considered.

However, this approach is very 'risk averse' and may be appropriate in the not-for-profit sector, and concentrates on recycling cash quickly.

CASE STUDY:
RENOWINDO LTD (2)

Consider again the two projects open to Renowindo Ltd, Projects A and B. Using RCI shows the anticipated incomes for the year 2006 as £25,000 and £5,000 respectively. This gives Project A a total six-year forecast return of £100,000 and Project B £80,000.

By using payback period as a method of deciding between investment projects, the choice made would be for Project B, as the payback would occur sometime early in 2003 for Project B as opposed to at the end of 2004 for Project A.

As can be seen, the total returns of £100,000 and £80,000 do not figure in the decision making process due to the criteria chosen by financial managers.

---

(3)   Discounted Cash Flow (DCF)

The start point for DCF is to acknowledge that the value of money changes over time, and a necessary requirement in calculating future revenues is access to Present Value Tables. These tables are necessary to allow the computation of the present financial value of a project based on the future cost or value of project returns. From a financial management standpoint, capital budgeting is used in project planning and appraisal in order to evaluate the benefits to be accrued from the commitment of financial resources in the long term.

The benefit to the organization of analysing future investment decisions will depend upon the quality of the information used in projecting the future. A major undertaking therefore has to be the calculation of the cost of capital to be used at a discounted rate in relation to cash flows. As an example, if £100 is invested today for five years at an interest rate of 5%, it would have a value of £127.63 in five years' time. Conversely, if you loan a friend £100 and he pays back £100 in five years (also at 5% interest), the Present Value of that £100 five years hence would only be £77.38.

Financial Performance

A further advantage of DCF is that it considers the forecast total life of the project, rather than choosing some simple mathematical expedient such as averages, over a shorter term in respect of returns. This method concentrates on cash flow.

 **CASE STUDY:
RENOWINDO LTD (3)**

Reconsidering the projects at Renowindo Ltd, the anticipated cost of money over the time of the project has first to be established.

In forecasting financial events, it pays to err on the side of caution. Therefore the rate chosen by Renowindo's accountants will be 8% per annum (at a time when prevailing base lending rates are 5%). The Present Value computation will be as follows:

	RENOWINDO LTD				
	Forecast Investment Appraisal 2001 – 2006				
Year	PV=8%	Project A Earnings	PV Earnings	Project B Earnings	PV Earnings
2001	0.9259	£5,000	£4,630	£25,000	£23,148
2002	0.8573	£10,000	£8,753	£18,500	£15,860
2003	0.7938	£15,000	£11,907	£16,500	£13,098
2004	0.735	£20,000	£14,700	£10,000	£7,350
2005	0.6806	£25,000	£17,015	£5,000	£3,403
2006	0.6302	£25,000	£15,755	£5,000	£3,151
Totals		£100,000	£72,760	£80,000	£66,010
Capital Invested			£50,000		£50,000
Forecast Profitability = NPV			£22,760		£16,010

From the above Net Present Value (NPV) computations, the preferred project choice is Project A.

www.universal-manager.co.uk

The best option for an organization might not necessarily be the option that offers the greatest return over time. It might be the option that enables the organization to remain financially viable and meet its debt commitment.

A lack of understanding by managers of investment appraisal has meant that many companies have found to their cost that the pursuit of profit through overtrading has affected their cash flow and ultimately this has resulted in an inability to meet outstanding debts. Overtrading means trading beyond the level that can be supported by the organization's financial means or the market involved.

09-2

PAUSE TO REFLECT

Is there a 'right' investment appraisal technique, or do you select the technique that gives the most acceptable result? If so, on what basis is 'acceptable' defined?

09-3 MANAGING BUDGETS

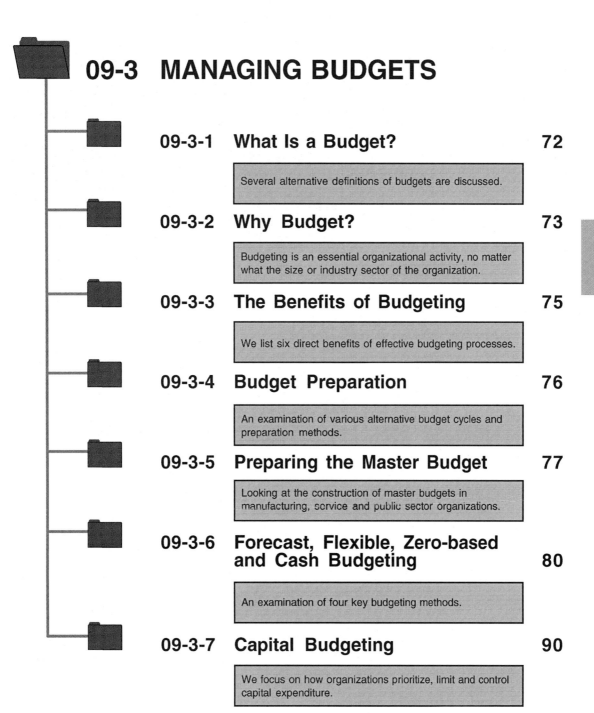

09-3

09-3 MANAGING BUDGETS

'The reason enlightened rulers and competent commanders win victories, achieve outstanding successes, and surpass ordinary people is that they know critical information in advance.'
(Donald G. Krause, 1995 after Sun Tzu, 500 BC)

09-3-1 What is a Budget?

In any organization the budget is a central aspect of the planning and control systems utilized by the organization. Regardless of the organization's size or complexity, or the product, the market or the service provided by the enterprise, a budget will always feature as a key aspect of financial planning.

The budget is always future oriented, but past performance of the organization, together with its strategic future expectations, will provide a framework in which to anticipate the utilization of the organization's resources.

> **Definition**
> A budget is a financial plan which details the ways in which the financial resource base of the organization will be allocated over a clear and specific time period — usually the financial year of the organization.

This is not a universal definition of a budget and other definitions include, for example:

☞ Any quantitative plan of action prepared in advance of the defined period of time.

☞ A management plan which shows the forecast resources required to achieve a strategy.

☞ A plan quantified in monetary terms, prepared and approved prior to a defined period of time, usually showing income, expenditure, capital employed, and objectives to be attained.

09-3-2   Why Budget?

Budgets represent the future strategies, goals, and objectives of an organization translated into financial terminology. However there are many other reasons why a budget system is both necessary and essential for any form of organizational activity. Consider the following case study.

CASE STUDY: CHILD CARE AND DEVELOPMENT

CHILD CARE AND DEVELOPMENT

09-3

A voluntary organization called Child Care and Development (CCD) was established within a local authority area in the South East of England. Its aim was to offer help and advice to single parents and to asylum seekers, many of whom could not speak English as their first language.

Although CCD was non-profit making, it had a strategy to break even, and therefore had to go through the processes of budgeting and financial resource management.

This organization faced many challenges, most of which were driven by the external environment, such as:

☞   The social trend of an increasing number of teenage pregnancies
☞   The political policy of the government *vis-à-vis* asylum seekers
☞   Human rights.

These challenges manifested themselves in the delays encountered by the management team between submitting financial bids to various groups and actually receiving the cash. At times the delay was more than a year from the drafting and submission of a bid, to the approval and receipt of grant money.

The various outside bodies that this voluntary organization had to contact to receive possible funding included the following:

☞   Children in Need
☞   The Local Education Authority, and other departments of the local authority
☞   Central government
☞   The Lottery Fund
☞   The Sports Council.

Further problems encountered were in relation to the substantial increase in the number of asylum seekers, and the potential for even more applicants arriving from war-torn regions of Eastern Europe and Africa. The financial planning system in the grants application process was, and will be, severely tested, due to the vast increase in potential clients for an overstretched voluntary budget. Close day-to-day monitoring against budgets is fundamentally important for CCD.

This real case study illustrates that not-for-profit organizations face similar challenges to businesses when it comes to managing financial performance. In this case, the local, national and political environments had (and are having) a direct impact on the day-to-day work of the managers responsible for the financial performance of this local charity. These particular influences may not be significant to some organizations. Other organizations may have other pressures on their financial performance such as exchange rates, supplier prices, the impact of technology, and so on. The need to apply similar techniques of financial management will still exist.

 ACTIVITY 9

The organization that you work for should have some form of budgetary system in place. Within your own organization, how is the budgeting process integrated with:

☛ Organizational goals?

☛ Decision making within the organization?

☛ Information and communication methods and channels?

☛ Organizational ethos and values?

☛ Reporting and monitoring systems?

The rest of this dossier will consider these challenges.

09-3-3   The Benefits of Budgeting

The following list, which is by no means exhaustive, covers many of the reasons why corporate activity benefits from the introduction of effective and efficient budgeting systems.

☞   Budgets are a specific and efficient way of supporting the co-ordination of many varied activities, both functional (in terms of tasks required to be performed) and organizational (in terms of the hierarchical structures within the organization).

☞   Budgets may be used to assist in the process of communicating organizational goals and aspirations to all levels.

☞   As the budget is a planning tool, the corporate budget will determine the various incomes and expenditures required within a particular time frame in order to achieve corporate goals.

☞   Budgets enable managers to plan for the future and take corrective action through anticipating problems.

☞   Financial budgets clearly quantify organizational objectives in financial terms, and also help to clearly identify areas of organizational priority.

☞   An effective budget control system will give clear indications to budget holders or cost centre managers as to the limits of their financial expenditure and the nature of that activity.

As a budget is not only an aspect of planning but also of control, frequent and timely budget monitoring will act as a control on expenditure and, importantly, measure actual performance against the budgeted plan.

ACTUAL	£20	£20
BUDGET	£19.95	£20.05
VARIANCE	£0.05	(£0.05)
	Happiness	Misery

(After Mr Micawber, *David Copperfield*, Charles Dickens.)

PAUSE TO REFLECT

Which of the following features of an organizational budget can be seen to work positively as advantages to your organization?

☞ Co-ordination of resources
☞ Improved communication within the organization
☞ Strategic planning through financial objectives
☞ Control through financial monitoring
☞ Involvement of staff at all levels
☞ Managerial motivation due to clear goals.

Are there any barriers to these potential advantages?

09-3-4   Budget Preparation

The budget represents the translation of an organization's future strategic plans into financial terms and measures. However, the budget is also a planning tool that is based on the best forecasts of what might happen in the future, and even the best laid plans of any organization can suffer from unpredictable events.

It is essential that managers who are involved in the budget preparation process have access to data that contains information concerning past performance in areas relating to revenue and expenditure. With the rapid increase in the development and utilization of information technology, the financial history of an organization can be examined both quickly and in great detail.

Organizations with knowledge management systems should be well placed to access such data with ease. However, knowledge management systems are often built around the technical aspects of product development or on customer and market information. The wise financial manager will see to it that financial modelling systems are integrated into such knowledge management systems where possible.

Another area where information communication technology assists budget preparation is the use of the internet or intranets. Not only can external information (for example, on local and national taxation rates, interest and borrowing rate fluctuations, exchange rates, and so on) be obtained quickly and easily, but benchmark data in industrial sectors is available; corporate financial data is readily available since many corporate web sites make their financial data available to current and would-be investors.

The usual time for budget preparation within an organization will in most cases be during the annual business planning cycle, so that the organization is financially prepared and organized before the financial or calendar year begins.

Budget preparation is an iterative process and must itself be monitored and controlled — without proper direction and control, it can be never-ending. For example, it may be that revenue forecasts can only be achieved by installing new production equipment, expanding the sales force, etc. This will require adjustments to capital expenditure budgets and overhead cost budgets. Conversely, overhead cost budgets that do not support the revenue forecast may lead to a forecast loss and/or intolerable negative cash flow. Cash forecasts themselves are prepared last since they impact on other cost budgets in terms of bank and interest charges.

The cycle for local authorities to plan and prepare their budgets can be as long as ten months from the preparation of the draft budget to final approval by the local council. This is due to the many and varied committee structures involved in local government processes and procedures.

In conventional business the budget, as with any other tool in the armoury of business planning, must be constantly monitored so that change can be implemented rapidly and effectively.

 ## 09-3-5   Preparing the Master Budget

Introduction

We will shortly consider an example of the budget preparation process — a manufacturing enterprise called 'Bunty's Boxes' which we first mentioned in section 09-2-4. Budget preparation for organizations in the service industries or in the public sector will show many similarities of concept but there will be differences.

Today, for example, companies such as Freeserve and AltaVista in the internet service provider (ISP) market place construct their budget programmes using the basic 'Master Budget' format. This format considers financial commitment on expenditure over a time frame which is short-term, but it anticipates the financial benefits to be accrued in the long-term. At the time of writing, the London and New York financial markets were still undecided as to whether the budgets of the dot-com stocks are realistic. In the middle of 2000, the euphoria surrounding the over-valuation of these stocks was beginning to subside with calls by financial analysts for basic business disciplines to be applied, i.e. that profits must be generated through real income within a reasonable period of time like any retail business. 'Reasonableness' will vary significantly between investments, for example as between a tangible and traditional project such as the Channel Tunnel and an intangible and innovative project such as Amazon.com.

On the other hand, organizations in the voluntary sector will be less likely to be in complete control of their own destiny, as they are subjected to the vagaries of political decisions and social expedients. They are unlike companies and businesses who can carefully and thoroughly research their future product/service/market situation and pursue their strategy with relative freedom.

Starting Points

Whether the organization is operating in the voluntary sector, the public sector, in the high-tech markets, or in a general business sector, the starting point for any budget will be the strategic plan of the organization which will anticipate any future incomes based on:

☞ Knowledge of the market and/or the environment
☞ The strengths and weaknesses inherent within the organization in terms of resources
☞ The opportunities for and threats to the organization.

From the strategic plan, the management will articulate the objectives of the organization. Some of these objectives will be financial and most will have financial implications.

The master budget will have as its start point the sales and income/revenue targets forecast in the strategic planning process. The master budget's composition will be determined by the area of operation of the organization, e.g. manufacturing or retail. The following definitions explain some of the factors involved.

(1) Definitions

Direct labour is the human resource cost directly associated with the manufacture of a particular product. For example, the cost of a production worker would be a direct labour cost, whereas the cost of a supervisor might be considered as an overhead cost.

Direct overheads are items such as the hire of some specialized equipment for use directly in the manufacturing process of a specific product.

Direct material cost would be all materials used in the manufacturing process, such as the raw materials and machinery used in the manufacturing of the specific product.

(2)   Manufacturing industries

The sales/revenue forecast will be built up first, in line with the organization's objectives. This will determine what production output is required which informs the manufacturing budget. This will consist of separate control budgets for direct labour, direct material costs and sundry manufacturing overheads. The budgets for overhead costs would then be built up, and once all budgets are in place, adjustments may be required. For example, additional capital expenditure may be required to support the production output required. This would necessitate a capital expenditure budget which would have an impact on financial overhead cost budgets.

09-3

(3)   Service industries

Service companies will also start with a sales/revenue forecast, but there are differences in the cost budgets as these companies do not have a manufacturing operation. Retailers, for example, would utilize a purchasing budget in place of a manufacturing budget. A purchasing budget determines the stock ranges and product lines to be purchased from the various suppliers of the retail organization, to ensure that consumer demand is satisfied, and that the strategic financial objectives of the organization are properly achieved.

Retail organizations will adopt such a budget system in order to meet objectives such as:

☞   Development of a wider consumer demand base
☞   Achievement of sales/profitability targets
☞   Reinforcement of consumer loyalty
☞   Stability in a volatile market place
☞   Increase in market share.

(4)   Public sector

In the public sector, the general starting point in the budget preparation process is the determination of the revenue budget. The revenue budget will detail the levels of income and expenditure forecasted for the next financial period, and from this the local authority can plan the levels of taxes and/or charges to be levied. Once the revenue budget has been agreed, the local authority can then plan its income and expenditure policies.

Organizations in the public sector might also develop their budgets in terms of clients, as is the case in the health service, or by the nature of particular projects, as might be the case with a local authority considering a new street lighting project, or a traffic calming project.

PAUSE TO REFLECT

It is of paramount importance that the sales forecasting, or situational forecasting methodology utilized by the organization results in an accurate revenue forecast. The sales budget, as previously discussed, and its equivalent in other organizations, is the basis of all subsequent budgets. Do all managers in your organization know what the sales/revenue forecast is for their functional area? How far have these figures been communicated? Is there belief in their attainability?

09-3-6 Forecast, Flexible, Zero-based and Cash Budgeting

The three major budgeting approaches are:

☛ The forecast (or fixed) budget
☛ The flexible budget
☛ The zero-based budget.

The first two are illustrated in the Bunty's Boxes case study.

The Forecast Budget

The forecast or fixed budget planner says:

> 'In line with our objectives and our market research, we forecast revenue of £100M this year. Historically, our cost of sales has been 40%. Our production/purchasing budgets are therefore . . . . We also forecast a gross margin of £60M. In order to deliver our revenue and achieve a 15% net profit our overhead costs total £45M as follows . . . .'

As with all budgets the forecast or fixed budget provides a basis for planning and co-ordinating an organization's business and financial activities. The main starting point for the forecast budget will be from the organization's historical data, i.e.:

- Previous budgets
- Previous financial statements
- Previous planning documents.

In smaller organizations, it may be as simple as using last year's spreadsheet with next year's data to extrapolate the budget. In larger organizations, and particularly with the increased pace of change, this approach is unlikely to be enough. The variables over short time frames will be too many and complex. Also, there is the problem that assumptions can become lost in sophisticated processing formulae — indeed sometimes financial forecasting on computers can become so complex that the fundamental assumptions become completely obscured. For example, an organization might have achieved a particular overall gross margin in the past and the software has been set up to work this out. But if the margin changes on one product line, will the planner remember to chase this change through to obtain the new overall margin? Perhaps changes might occur in average debtor days which need to be reflected in the next year's financial model; interest rates will fluctuate; and so on. Caution must be exercised in using the technology to extrapolate budgets in this way.

A major advantage of the forecast budget is that it provides a clear picture of the strategic financial wishes of the organization for the specific time period of the planned budget. Against this forecast, actual results can be clearly measured and variations can be analysed.

A drawback in the forecast budget is that it is rigid and inflexible in nature, and thus does not allow for adjustments to be made in consideration of changes in the volume of production, or in the demand for the product or service.

The Flexible Budget

The flexible budget planner says:

> 'In line with our objectives and our market research, we forecast revenue of £100M this year. However, there are some significant "what ifs" to consider meaning that revenue may fluctuate by 5% either way. Historically, our cost of sales has ranged been 30% and 40%. Our production/purchasing budgets need to be variable, etc. . . . . We therefore forecast a gross margin in the range £57–73.5M. In order to deliver our revenue and achieve a 20% net profit our overhead costs will be in the range £38-52.5M as follows . . . .'

The flexible budget is sometimes referred to as the control budget. The flexible budget recognizes the shortcomings of the fixed budget approach in terms of its basis in 'future estimates', and the inability of the fixed budget approach to handle change in the event of actual volumes differing from the budgeted volume figures.

In most business planning, a certain degree of 'guesstimation' takes place, as no business planner can accurately predict the actual future demand behaviour within the market place. It is therefore incumbent upon planners to consider 'ranges' of potential performance and budget accordingly within the bounds of these range figures.

The flexible budget is so designed as to take into account, at the budget planning stage, differences which might occur in costs, both fixed and variable, through changes in output volume and/or sales volume.

CASE STUDY: BUNTY'S BOXES (2)

The sales figures for the past two years have been as follows:

    1998   12,200 units
    1999   14,300 units

Bunty's Boxes has just launched a new website with an on-line 'design your own box' facility. This is expected to attract new customers, and volume sales are anticipated to be substantially higher in 2001 than in 2000.

Present manufacturing capacity at Bunty's Boxes is 20,000 units and the directors are anticipating sales volume to be within the range of 16,000 to 18,000 units. As there is a wide variance within the anticipated sales volume, the managing director has asked for a fixed master budget to be prepared at 17,000 units and flexible budgets to be prepared at 16,000 and 18,000 units respectively.

The first stage is to utilize known data to ascertain the variable cost per unit of production, as follows:

Year	Unit Sales	Income	Cost of Sales
2000	14,300	£171,600	£98,900
1999	12,200	£146,400	£88,400
Change	2,100	£25,200	£10,500

(The sales price per unit is £12.)

The variable cost per unit is calculated by dividing the variation in the number of units sold in the two periods (2,100) into the difference in the cost of sales during the same period (£10,500).

$$\frac{£10,500}{2,100} = £5 \; \textit{variable cost per unit of production}$$

The fixed costs can now be calculated as follows:

2000
Total cost of 14,300 units = £98,900
Variable cost of 14,300 units = 14,300 x £5 = £71,500
Fixed costs = £27,400

1999
Total cost of 12,200 units = £88,400
Variable cost of 12,200 units = 12,200 x £5 = £61,000
Fixed costs = £27,400

It can therefore be seen that the fixed costs for the two previous periods, 1999 and 2000, are the same and for this example the assumption will be that the fixed costs remain constant at £27,400.

Bunty's Boxes Budgets for 2001:

		Fixed Budget (17,000 units)	Flexible Budget (16,000 units)	Flexible Budget (18,000 units)
(a)	Sales @ £12	£204,000	£192,000	£216,000
(b)	Variable costs @ £5	£85,000	£80,000	£90,000
(c)	Contribution (a – b)	£119,000	£112,000	£126,000
(d)	Fixed costs	£27,400	£27,400	£27,400
(e)	Predicted Profit (c – d)	£91,600	£84,600	£98,600

The Bunty's Boxes flexible budget combined with a fixed budget prediction gives the organization a greater degree of predictability and therefore control over anticipated incomes and the expenses needed to achieve unit sales figures.

The combination of fixed and flexible budgets offers a number of advantages, such as:

☛ A wider range of managerial participation can take place, by outlining several budgetary scenarios rather than fixing on only one.

☛ Communications at all levels within the organization are encouraged, underlining the importance of a broad base of input to the decision making process.

☛ The higher the level of participation in the budgetary process, the greater the likelihood of a higher level of job satisfaction and motivation through a sense of 'ownership' of the process.

☛ The more people participating in the budgeting process, the greater the degree of accuracy in the final picture, as queries and problems can be ironed out through more enlightened, organizationally-based discussion.

Zero-based Budgeting

Zero-based budgeting is useful where:

☛ Revenue is fixed — it cannot be significantly increased and the hope is that it will not be decreased.
☛ The net profit & loss must be zero since surpluses cannot be used or carried forward, and deficits are intolerable.
☛ The organization does not have any historical data on expected revenue and costs, or the behaviour of both in relation to variations in operational performance.

Other forms of budgeting accommodate variations in both revenue and net profit & loss; these forms also utilize historical data. Zero-based budgeting is typically used:

☛ In not-for-profit organizations
☛ When an organization plans the introduction of a new operation, e.g. the manufacture and promotion of a new product.

In reality, most organizations will rarely use zero-based budgeting as the only budgeting process. This is partly because it takes much more time than other forms of budgeting and partly because many not-for-profit organizations will not rely solely on grants for revenue. Many public sector organizations have revenue-generating activities. So we see situations where:

☞ Zero-based budgeting is the organization's overall basis for budgeting, with other budgeting methods used for department budgets

☞ Other budgeting methods are the basis for overall budgeting, with zero-based budgeting used for specific projects.

Zero-based budgeting moves away completely from the ethos of following previous tried and tested financial models. Managers have to justify every single line and item of the budget, and measure the value of specific activities against untried alternatives.

09-3

To develop a zero-based budget there needs to be:

(1) A clear identification of cost or service centres. For example, in the Amenities Department of a local authority, the cost centres may include:

☞ Waste disposal
☞ Animal welfare
☞ Conservation
☞ Recycling
☞ Parks and leisure.

In a capital expenditure project in a business, the cost centres may include:

☞ Feasibility and investment appraisal.
☞ Project planning.
☞ Project implementation. This will in turn be broken down into any number of cost centres depending on the nature of the project. Particular phases might have their own master budgets. In building a road for example, this might be broken down into surveying, contracting, bridge building, groundworks, decking and surface laying, etc. Each phase will then have its own set of 'internal' budgets.
☞ Testing, proving and commissioning.

(2)   The development of decision criteria *vis-à-vis* budget allocation. For example, these might include:

☞   The benefits accrued to the local area through performance within a particular cost centre, i.e. the benefits to the community based on increasing the recycling budget

☞   The cost/benefit approach to spending more of the budget on one cost/service area than on another — dog wardens as opposed to street cleaning, for example

☞   Investment appraisal (see later).

(3)   Clear definition of fixed, variable and semi-variable costs. In a capital investment project, for example, some costs (e.g. interest) will vary according to time. The total of these costs should not exceed the planned capital expenditure amount as overspending could threaten the completion of the project.

(4)   What-if budgets. It is always wise to have what-if budgets, whatever the budgeting method. Zero-based budgets by definition have fixed limits and can be easily 'blown' by unplanned events. Delays, changes in costs during the budget period, or underachievement of outputs may reduce revenue availability or increase the cost of a project, for example. It is usual to carry out sensitivity tests by varying key cost lines related to the most likely unplanned events that will change the budget, e.g. interest rate changes, supplier cost changes, etc.

(5)   Identification and justification of contingency. A proportion of the budget must be allocated to contingency to accommodate unforeseen eventualities. The contingency budget will be informed by the results of the what-if budgets. The budget should also indicate how the contingency will be utilized in the event of an underspend.

As a methodology, zero-basing is costly and time consuming, and its usefulness within organizational planning has been recognized not as a budgetary tool but more as a technique to support the development of overall corporate strategy. The technique allows a wider time frame to be utilized, especially in sectors that are clearly influenced by political expedience.

 **ACTIVITY 10**

Considering your current position and what you have just read:

(1)   What budgetary planning techniques do you employ?

09-3

(2)   Is it time to reconsider the financial models used?

(3)   Would a zero-based technique benefit your organization in any way?

In the last activity, you may have mentioned cash budgeting. Read on to find out more.

The Cash Budget

The cash budget considers the various income and expenditure scenarios anticipated for a forthcoming period, and from this information corporate decisions concerning resource utilization will have to be made. The cornerstone of the cash budget is an analysis of income and expenditure over a specified period, culminating in the preparation of a cash flow statement, showing the cash situation month-by-month, whether positive or negative.

Typical of this process is the Galashields Gorillas ice hockey team.

In this example, the cash flow situation plays an important part in the final decisions to be taken by the owners of the ice hockey team with regard to the feasibility of progressing with the refurbishment package.

CASE STUDY: THE GALASHIELDS GORILLAS (2)

The Galashields Gorillas ice hockey team needs to consider its future in the light of its promotion to the Premier Division. It has to consider the implications of the £1M refurbishment required to bring it into line with the stadium requirements for Premier Division teams (see Activity 6 on page 53).

The following financial data is available for the six-month period January to June 2000:

(a) The club will have to pay the contractor as follows:
£500,000 on 1 January, £250,000 on 1 March and £250,000 on 1 May.

(b) The Galashields Borough Council will pay Galashields Gorillas £500,000 also on 1 March.

(c) A player will be sold in January for £70,000, another in February for £65,000, and finally one more in June for £48,000.

(d) Expenses on match days allocated to each month are shown in the following table, together with the anticipated receipts from matches played.

	January	February	March	April	May	June
Expenses	£16,500	£14,000	£17,500	£16,500	£13,600	£15,000
Receipts	£58,600	£52,200	£63,500	£56,000	£51,500	£61,400

(e) Fixed expenses for the club are £4,500 per month

(f) Variable expenses are half of the home game receipts and are settled one month in arrears.

(g) The receipts from home games in December 1999 were £64,000.

(h) The cash balance in the bank on 1 January 2000 is £134,600.

www.universal-manager.co.uk

The resulting cash budget looks like this:

Galashields Gorillas Ice Hockey Team						
Cash Budget — January to June 2000						
	January	**February**	**March**	**April**	**May**	**June**
RECEIPTS (£)						
Sale of players	70000	65000				48000
Game receipts	58600	52200	63500	56000	51500	61400
Local authority			500000			
TOTAL RECEIPTS (A)	128600	117200	563500	56000	51500	109400
OUTGOINGS £						
Refurbishment	500000		250000		250000	
Match expenses	16500	14000	17500	16500	13600	15000
Fixed expenses	4500	4500	4500	4500	4500	4500
Variable expenses	32000	29300	26100	31750	28000	25750
TOTAL OUTGOINGS (B)	553000	47800	298100	52750	296100	45250
NET CASH FLOW (A – B)	–424400	69400	265400	3250	–244600	64150
Opening balance	134600	–289800	–220400	45000	48250	–196350
Closing balance	–289800	–220400	45000	48250	–196350	–132200

09-3

As can be seen from the computation results, the closing bank balance at the end of June 2000 is negative, but does this mean that the project should be abandoned? The simple cash flow budgetary calculation should be used only as a guide, or a framework within which to examine other issues of a much wider nature.

With regard to the computation itself, one observation is that it is based on forecast projections which, based on historical data within the ice hockey club, may be somewhat on the conservative side. For example, it could be the case that the match receipts forecast has been based on the attendance figures and admission charges of previous seasons when the Gorillas were in a lower division, and these could easily be increased due to the new status of the club. Other income-producing factors such as sales of replica kits and memorabilia may also increase, more so than gate receipts. There may be an increase in television rights revenues and other off-the-field activities.

ACTIVITY 11

Imagine that you are presenting the financial report to the January meeting of the club's Board of Directors, based on this cash budget. What would be the main points that you would make?

Refer to Appendix 1 for commentary.

PAUSE TO REFLECT

The case study illustrates the point that the figures by themselves are not important — although ensuring their accuracy is essential. The important point is how the figures inform management decisions, and how management decisions are then taken on the basis of the available figures.

If you were Chairman of Galashields Gorillas and you were meeting the bank manager, what message would you be aiming to put across?

09-3-7 Capital Budgeting

Most organizations operate some sort of capital budgeting process. Unless capital is unlimited there will be some need for budgeting. The formality of the process varies from organization to organization. Size is not the most important factor in driving the formalization of the process. Although larger organizations are likely to have formal processes at all levels, it is important for smaller organizations to have a clear policy with regard to their capital activities.

Capital budgeting, as the term suggests, is concerned with setting limits on capital expenditure. At the least formal end of the scale, the approach would be merely to assess whether the expenditure required by a project is affordable. The quality of the assessment itself will determine the success of this case-by-case approach. The more formal approach is to set annual capital budgets. The budget figure either represents the maximum amount of capital available within that financial year, or the suggested ceiling — which may be raised if assessment shows that the benefits are worthwhile. The 'set in stone' budget figure is referred to as a *hard ceiling* constraint. The flexible figure represents a *soft ceiling*.

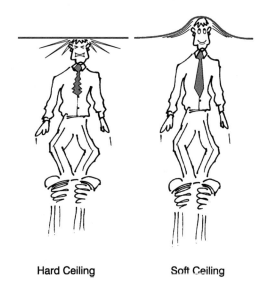

Hard Ceiling   Soft Ceiling

The capital budget figure may be sub-divided so that there are limits set to control the percentages of the total that any one project can call on. No one project can use more than 30% of the total, for example. The budget may also be governed by strategic factors. The organization may set its budget along investment category lines. Investments can be split into three types:

☞   Growth investments
☞   Replacement and maintenance investments
☞   Cost-reduction investments.

Growth investments include expansion and diversification investments. Expansion investments increase the size and/or efficiency of the manufacture of existing (or similar) products with the aim of increasing sales. Diversification is the movement into new products or new territories, or both.

Replacement and maintenance investments can be divided into two types:

☞   The 'must do's', e.g. because they are legislative requirements such as health and safety requirements.
☞   The 'nice to do's', e.g. redecorating the offices.

From a financial viewpoint, these investments can be broken down into two types:

☞ Those with tangible costs and benefits that can be measured. For example, the cost of maintaining production plant is easily quantified. The benefits in terms of maintaining production capacity/levels are similarly easy to quantify. There is also another benefit which cannot be measured in financial terms: that of maintaining operators' morale which will be higher if their machinery is not constantly breaking down.

☞ Those that cannot be measured. Complying with health and safety legislation, for example, presents some difficulties in financial terms. Costs are not always the simple cost of replacement or installation. For example, installing machine guards may incur the cost of slowing down production. The benefit is that operators are less likely to be maimed, and consequently the business is less likely to end up in court defending both criminal and civil actions. Reduced insurance premiums may, however, be a quantifiable benefit.

Consider the example of a business that has to install anti-pollution cleaning equipment in its fume/exhaust extraction system. This can be immensely costly and have no tangible benefit other than that the business will not be prosecuted by the enforcement authorities. There have been cases where plant managers have decided to close down the business because their investment appraisal showed clearly that the capital and maintenance expenditure required made the business non-viable.

 PAUSE TO REFLECT

Sometimes, managers argue strongly for replacement capital expenditure with no financially quantifiable benefit. Have you encountered situations where this is the case, and the reasons could be classified as:

☞ Personal — individual preference — boosts/maintains perceptions of individual self-image?

☞ Personnel — staff morale, facilitating recruitment, working conditions, organizational self-image, etc.?

☞ Strategic marketing — external image, PR, political positioning, branding?

---

www.universal-manager.co.uk

Cost reduction investments are designed to save money by making the organization more efficient and profitable. This might be achieved through investments in new machinery and technology. More usually these days, these investments relate to reorganization arising from:

- The need for constant innovation
- The need for organizations to reinvent or re-engineer themselves
- Competitive pressure
- Introduction of new systems such as knowledge management systems.

When these investments are assessed it is important that they are assessed in both the short and the long term. There may come a time in the life of an investment where it no longer looks so attractive, and, by the end of its life, may ultimately be more expensive than other initially more expensive options. When considering these types of investments the less tangible consequences and costs need to be considered. For example, the costs of retraining and adapting to new technology have to be included or estimated. These might include:

09-3

- Costs of the organization's training staff
- Costs of external suppliers — training consultants, resources (books, videos, etc.)
- Travelling, subsistence and venue costs
- Opportunity costs — the costs of an employee not doing his/her job (lost sales, lost production, etc.)

The effect on morale of changes in working methods has to be carefully assessed before major upheavals are undertaken. These factors can have a major bearing on the ultimate success of any capital investment of this nature.

The capital budget will typically be allied to a strategic aim. The strategic aim, where the organization wants to be, will dictate, to a large extent, the nature of the organization's investments. The capital budget will therefore reflect the areas that coincide with the strategic aim. If the organization's strategic aim is growth oriented, then the investments will be growth oriented. When considering the proposals put before them senior management should bear in mind these factors, as well as remembering the necessity to keep aside sufficient capital to fund the requirements of on-going projects and investments. The organization will also probably need to make some replacement and maintenance investments, and some in cost reduction too. The management committee that makes these decisions has to be clear on the policies that lie behind their decisions.

They need to be able to assess the proposals put before them objectively and arrive at a planned investment that maximizes returns while satisfying strategic aims, ensuring that all projects and investments undertaken are properly supported and amply budgeted for.

In a vibrant organization, there are always more projects than capital available to fund them. One of the most important roles for senior managers is to prioritize projects to support strategy, and to ensure that they are adequately funded. Indeed, performance in this area defines the difference between success and failure for senior management teams.

PAUSE TO REFLECT

The costs of recruitment, selection and training of personnel are often aligned to capital expenditure. Are there any occasions when your organization budgets for these costs as capital expenditure, or are they routinely allocated to cost/overhead budgets? Ask your organization's financial managers.

www.universal-manager.co.uk

CASE STUDY:
THE XYZ COMPANY

The XYZ Company is looking at its investment opportunities. It has a capital budget for the year of £500,000. It is faced with the task of selecting the best combination of investments from those put before it. In reaching this decision the strategic aims of the business need to be kept in mind, as well as shorter-term objectives.

XYZ Company has strategic aims which require some growth investment. It also needs to invest in replacement and maintenance to keep its operation running efficiently. It would like to invest in cost-cutting projects but realizes that at this time this is not the highest priority.

Proposed Investments (capital required)

Growth Investments		*Repair and Maintenance Investments*	
Project 1	£100,000	Project 1	£70,000
Project 2	£78,000	Project 2	£100,000
Project 3	£55,000	Project 3	£44,000
Project 4	£130,000	Project 4	£33,000
Project 5	£223,000		

Cost Reduction Investments
Project 1	£40,000
Project 2	£115,000
Project 3	£28,000
Project 4	£200,000

 ACTIVITY 12

From the above data select the projects that you think should be chosen to best reflect the organization's strategic aims and its budget limitations. (The projects are ranked in order of their net benefit, i.e. the resulting benefit minus the cost: so Project 1 is more attractive in net benefit terms than Project 2 and so on.)

See Appendix 1 for commentary.

09-4 COSTING TECHNIQUES

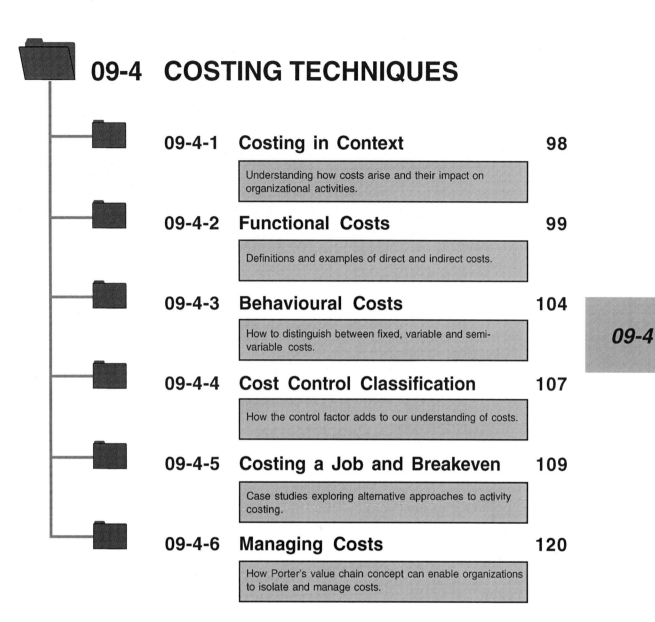

09-4

09-4 COSTING TECHNIQUES

*'Estimating completely creates victory. Estimating
incompletely causes failure. When we look at it from this
point of view, it is obvious who will win the war.'*
(Donald G. Krause, 1995 after Sun Tzu, 500 BC)

09-4-1 Costing in Context

Understanding cost is an essential function of management. Perhaps the least complex costs to understand are the costs of manufacture - raw materials, direct labour and overheads. Harder to understand and manage are other costs such as marketing and service costs. Even more difficult to understand are competitors' costs. In this section, we will look mainly at the first set of costs.

A cost is any aspect of the activity of an organization that has a price to be paid by that organization. The term 'cost' in the business environment can be interpreted in a variety of ways. Its interpretation will be refined in order that a cost can be attributable to a specific activity, function or process of the organization in the furtherance of its objectives.

Cost is arguably the most important element of price. There are two general issues for managers which flow from this. One issue concerns how costs (and consequently prices in some cases) are reported. The other issue is that unless clear models are used for identifying costs, an organization will find it difficult to operate on a financially viable basis.

With regard to the first issue, there is an ethical dimension illustrated by many examples in the UK where the Monopolies and Mergers Commission (MMC) has taken action because price fixing has been alleged. Areas that have been investigated (or are under investigation at the time of writing) by the MMC or other quangos are petrol prices, milk prices, car prices and book prices, to mention but a few. Price fixing usually arises where a few suppliers or distributors are dominant in the marketplace (in a monopoly position). In the late twentieth century, price fixing also occurred (in an attempt to create a market) with the regulation of privatized public utilities — railways, water supply and so on. In all these cases, there have been questions about the ethical stance of the management of the organizations involved:

☞ Have they exploited their customers and suppliers as a result of market dominance?
☞ Have they priced their products and services fairly?
☞ Have they reported their costs accurately?

How organizations in this kind of position calculate, apportion and report their costs is a matter for ethical financial management. Clearly, in the public sector, local government officers (for example) have a duty to be transparent about the way in which costs are calculated and apportioned. Although their work is subject to regular public scrutiny, it is not unknown for costs in public sector organizations (in all countries) to be 'managed' in order not to lose budget (and therefore control or power) in the following financial year although 'carry-overs' are becoming more accepted.

PAUSE TO REFLECT

Are there occasions when managers are justified in taking action to 'defend' their cost budgets in order to retain control within an organization?

09-4

The following section looks at the second issue mentioned previously, namely that of identifying and applying appropriate costing models.

09-4-2   Functional Costs

In any manufacturing organization, whether it produces cat food or cars, the functional way that costs are categorized will be in terms of:

☞   Direct costs

☞   Indirect costs.

Direct costs are defined as those costs that are associated directly with the manufacturing and production processes of the organization. The three main components of direct cost are:

☞   Direct labour

☞   Direct materials

☞   Direct expenses.

These are sometimes referred to collectively as 'Prime Costs'.

All other costs are classified as indirect — sometimes referred to as 'overheads'.

Financial Performance

To examine these categories consider the following short corporate case study of Renowindo Ltd.

CASE STUDY:
RENOWINDO LTD (4)

Renowindo is a small family business, and cost management is a major priority. For proper financial control, it is essential to allocate all costs into direct and indirect cost classifications.

During the financial year 1998 – 1999 the following data was available for analysis into cost classification:

Renowindo Ltd 1998 – 1999

Corporate Data

The organization employs the following personnel at its Gravesend manufacturing unit:

- ☛ 2 supervisors
- ☛ 12 skilled glaziers/fitters
- ☛ 3 trainee glaziers/fitters.

The supervisors were each paid £22,000 during 1998 –1999, and the total wage bill for the skilled glaziers/fitters amounted to £192,000 for the same period. The three trainees were partly subsidized from central government employment grants through a Modern Apprenticeship Scheme. However, Renowindo still had to pay £16,500 in total to the trainees.

Also employed at the Gravesend unit were:

- ☛ 1 organization secretary/accountant
- ☛ 1 receptionist
- ☛ 2 secretaries
- ☛ 1 clerical assistant/office junior.

The total salary bill for the administrative staff for the period 1998 – 1999 amounted to £82,000.

www.universal-manager.co.uk

During the trading year 1998 – 1999, materials required to construct the double glazing windows and doors cost the organization £368,000, and due to a special, non-standard order, a specialist machine was hired at a cost of £46,000. Other costs incurred by Renowindo during this period were:

☛ Rental of premises (£168,000) of which £100,000 was factory space and £68,000 was office accommodation.

☛ Other manufacturing costs such as electricity (£34,000).

Renowindo Ltd employs a sales team who are paid on a commission-only basis. During 1998 – 1999 commission paid amounted to £126,000.

Other cost groupings were as follows:

☛ Administration (telephone, stationery, etc.)   £24,500
☛ Advertising   £38,000

09-4

Finally, for the period 1998 – 1999, Renowindo achieved sales of £1,888,500.

Read our commentary on this case study on the next page.

Commentary on Case Study

Using this data, we can carry out a functional cost classification as follows:

(1) Direct costs

(a) *Direct labour costs*

Direct labour costs are the wages paid to the skilled fitters and the trainees, £192,000 and £16,500 respectively, as these employees contribute totally to the production of the various products manufactured and sold.

(Total = £208,500)

(b) *Direct materials cost*

Direct materials are those materials used in the manufacturing process — the costs incurred by Renowindo to purchase materials from which to manufacture the double glazing units.

(Total = £368,000)

(c) *Direct expenses*

Direct expenses are accrued specifically in the production process of the double glazing products. In this case the hire of specialist equipment to be used to produce a special order is categorized as a direct expense.

(Total = £46,000)

(2) Indirect costs

All of the other costs incurred during the year 1998 – 1999 are indirect costs.

(a) Factory costs

Factory overhead includes the salaries of the supervisors at £44,000, as the supervisors do not work 'hands-on' in production but supervise and ensure that staffing issues (for example) are properly dealt with. Also in this category is the cost of premises, which can be used for other activities such as office space for the supervisors, toilets, canteen facilities, etc., at a cost of £100,000. Finally in this classification is the cost of electricity, which although used in the production process is not solely used for this purpose, at £34,000.

(Total = £178,000)

09-4

(b) Administration costs

A further category of indirect cost is those costs associated with the administration function of Renowindo. During the year 1998 – 1999 these expenses were made up as follows:

☞ Salaries of administrative personnel, £82,000
☞ Premises cost, £68,000
☞ Administrative expenses, £24,500.

(Total = £174,500)

(c) Selling costs

The last indirect cost is those expenses associated with the sales and promotion of the various double glazing products, these being sales commission of £126,000 and advertising costs of £38,000.

(Total = £164,000)

ACTIVITY 13

Given the functional cost analysis for Renowindo for 1998 – 1999, calculate the gross margin and net margin for the period.

Refer to Appendix 1 for a commentary before continuing.

09-4-3 Behavioural Costs

Another way of looking at any costs incurred by an organization is to consider the cost on the basis of the way in which the cost element might change or vary according to changes in the level or volume of activity. Behavioural cost classifications are:

☞ Fixed Costs

☞ Variable Costs

☞ Semi-variable Costs.

Fixed Costs

A cost incurred by an organization is considered a fixed cost if it remains fairly constant in total during a specific and predetermined time period such as a financial year. During this period, the cost will not change even though the level of organizational activity may change. Examples of fixed costs include:

- Rental of premises, vehicles, computers, etc.
- Rates
- Salaries (provided they are not tied into bonus or commission schemes)
- Depreciation.

Variable Costs

Variable costs are those costs that will change in direct proportion to changes in the related activity level. In other words, the cost of the single item or unit will remain constant but the total cost of the items or unit will rise and fall depending upon changes in the level of demand.

09-4

For example, if Renowindo utilized a specific type of casement lock for a window, the costs involved in charging for the installation of the window would include fitting the casement lock. The cost per lock would remain constant whether five or six windows were sold. However the total cost of locks would increase in response to the volume change in activity from five to six.

Semi-variable Costs

These are sometimes referred to as 'mixed costs' as they are made up of component parts of both fixed and variable costs. Examples of semi-variable costs incurred by an organization would include utilities such as gas and electricity, whose charges will comprise both a fixed charge for the basic service and a charge which varies according to usage. A common example is a salesman's salary which is made up of a basic wage and commission.

Financial Performance

Phone bills are another example of semi-variable costs. Land lines are usually billed as line rental (fixed) and call charges (variable); mobiles are sometimes billed as service (fixed) and call charges (variable); and internet services may include a more complex mix, such as:

☞ ISP charges — if not free, usually fixed in relation to server space rented or the number of e-mail addresses required.

☞ Dial-up access — currently variable as call charges are billed, but some companies (particularly in the USA) charge a fixed monthly fee and call charges are free.

☞ Information services — CompuServe, for example, acts as a 'free' ISP, but charges a monthly subscription for its information services plus additional charges for premium services and excess internet access time.

There is an increasing tendency in the telecommunications market to sell 'bundled' deals — a monthly subscription for line rental and call charges combined. This makes accounting easier (it's a recurring fixed cost) but these deals may not be good value.

The actual allocation of the costs will show as a separate line in the cost overview, rather than as a contribution to both fixed and variable.

 ACTIVITY 14

(1) Make a list of the main costs relating to your organization (or department if it's easier). Then categorize them into the following cost categories:

☞ Fixed
☞ Variable
☞ Semi-variable.

www.universal-manager.co.uk

(2)   Also, consider and investigate the effects that 'new technologies' have had within your organization or organizational cost centre.

   (a)   Have they added to costs, reduced costs or not affected costs much?
   (b)   Which costs have been most affected by the new technologies - fixed, variable or semi-variable?
   (c)   Are the costs of the new technologies well under control in your organization, or do they have a voracious appetite for cash?

09-4

Now read on.

 ## 09-4-4   Cost Control Classification

Finally, in this overview of cost classification, there is a method of determining cost as either

☞   Controllable or
☞   Non-controllable.

Controllable Costs

A controllable cost is one which the organization can directly determine and manage. An example of controllable cost might be the salary bill for administrative staff. Over a predetermined time period, the number of staff and the salary rate will generally remain constant and may be varied by management as necessary. Similarly, the rate at which depreciation is factored in to the asset value of an organization would be controllable by corporate management, usually advised by accountants or auditors.

Non-controllable Costs

This category comprises all costs beyond the control of corporate management. Examples of non-controllable costs would include the price of raw materials from suppliers, and changes in corporate taxation systems. It is essential for organizations to have as much control as possible over costs, otherwise the budgeting and planning processes will be driven by external variances, which could have a negative effect on product/service demand and profitability. In financial management, we think of variances as the differences between what is planned and what actually happens. For example, an organization may gear up its production based on projected sales expectations of 100,000 units. If actual sales only reach 90,000 units, the shortfall variance will impact on the 'per unit' cost and corporate profitability.

 ACTIVITY 15

Look again at the costs for your own department or organization and use the above classification techniques to analyse where the costs of your department/organization are deployed.

(1) What is the correlation between your analysis and the allocation of cost centres and/or budgets?

(2) Do budget holders manage a mix of cost types, or do some budget holders only manage variable costs?

(3) Does the mix of cost classification impact on the way in which that part of the organization is managed?

Now read on.

Summary

Managing financial performance in any organization requires that costs are properly considered, i.e. that they are appropriately classified and correctly calculated. Astute managers will anticipate and analyse 'cost traps' and thus 'design them out' of financial models. It is also of paramount importance that managers work to influence non-controllable costs to the benefit of the organization. This will involve close teamworking between financial, operational, purchasing and marketing managers.

09-4

 ## 09-4-5 Costing a Job and Breakeven

Before costing a job, it is essential that everyone concerned with the job understands exactly what it is. A job could start directly from a client, customer, consumer, or user, or from the organization's expectation of the way in which the anticipated customer will react within a specific market. A job could be any one of the following:

☞ An individual bespoke product such as a tailored suit
☞ A specific batch of similar products such as tins of baked beans
☞ A service such as that provided by a legal firm, for example, making out a will
☞ A major construction project such as the Channel Tunnel, the high-speed rail link from the Channel Tunnel to London, and so on
☞ A production line of cars
☞ An order for double glazing a house.

In many organizations the type of product will determine the way in which the production method takes place, and consequently the way in which costing occurs. However, in financial management the distinctions between *costing* methods should not be confused with different types of *production* methods. It is worth noting the basic types of production since they have different implications for costing purposes:

☞ **Jobbing Production** — a 'one-off' type of production, developed for one specific customer. Examples of this production method would be the construction of a bridge or dam, writing a computer program, or developing an advertising campaign for the product or service of an individual client.

☞ **Batch Production** — products that are produced in substantial quantities in one discrete run because a limited number is required, or because the production process must be stopped before replenishing/refreshing. This book is an example of a batch production method, where a number of books were produced to satisfy demand. Another batch of books will be printed when the previous batch is sold. Other examples of batch production would include paint manufacturers producing batches of colours, and food manufacturers producing batches of sausages.

☞ **Flow Production** — used where there is continuous demand for the end product and the production process does not need to be stopped for replenishing or refreshment. Flow production can be seen in fluid production — gas and oils for example. However many everyday items such as 'white goods' and vehicles are produced in a basic flow production system.

CASE STUDY: BREWING IN THE UK

An interesting example is the brewing business whose 'real ale' customers eschew beers and lagers produced by continuous flow. A good bitter beer (such as that produced in traditional English breweries or the countless microbreweries in the USA) is brewed in batches; so too is a traditional German lager which should stand for up to three months in a 'lager' before bottling. However, the multinational drinks conglomerates, in pursuit of greater efficiency, have established continuous flow production plants which produce barrels of beer and lager at lower unit cost than batch production.

www.universal-manager.co.uk

One financial consequence of this is that the brewers have to discount their product to retailers (pubs, bars, etc.) in times of low demand. This is because production capacity is geared to times of peak demand — generally holiday seasons. Thus student bars in colleges and universities are able to sell beer at low prices since their peak demand occurs during term-time when brewers experience demand below their production capacity.

CASE STUDY : RENOWINDO LTD (5)

09-4

Renowindo Ltd (see earlier for business description) deals with individual orders rather than a standardized product. It therefore uses the 'Jobbing' or 'Job Costing' system. As this is the case, all jobs at the organization will commence after the receipt of an order from a client.

The process at Renowindo is as follows:

- ☛ Customer order received from sales team
- ☛ Order acknowledged and confirmed
- ☛ Job estimated in terms of labour, materials, expenses, and overheads
- ☛ Job costing sheet produced (see pro forma)
- ☛ Job now 'work in progress'
- ☛ Job completed, cost summary sheet produced (see pro forma).

As can be seen from the above mentioned stages, the costing of the job will be clear and specific. However, on occasions the labour rate may be adjusted for a rush order which might mean that overtime rates have to be paid. In general the cost of labour will be computed as:

Standard Labour Pay Rate x Hours Worked

Similarly, materials used will be costed as:

Items Used x Quantity x Unit Cost

Any special direct expenses, such as the hire of specialist equipment, will also be costed in.

RENOWINDO LTD

JOB COSTING SHEET

Job Ref. No.:   Job start:

Customer Ref. No.:

Product Ref. No.:   Job end:

Direct Materials Required:

Part number	Quantity	Cost/unit	Total Cost

TOTAL DIRECT MATERIALS COST:

Direct Labour Required:

Skill area	Hours	Hourly rate	Total Cost

TOTAL DIRECT LABOUR COST:

Direct Expenses Required:

Category	Quantity		Total Cost

TOTAL DIRECT EXPENSES:

Overhead Requirements:

Indirect Expense	Quantity	Rate	Total Cost

TOTAL INDIRECT OVERHEAD:

RENOWINDO LTD

COST SUMMARY SHEET

Job Ref. No.:

Customer Ref. No.:

Product Ref. No.:

COST CENTRES	TOTAL COST (£)
TOTAL DIRECT MATERIALS	
TOTAL DIRECT LABOUR	
TOTAL DIRECT EXPENSES	
TOTAL INDIRECT OVERHEAD	
TOTAL JOB COST	

09-4

The cost of overheads will generally be averaged over the year based on past experience. Therefore every job will be charged a 'contribution cost' at a fixed rate, rather than attempt to determine the actual electricity used, administration required, or sales effort needed to obtain the order.

As can be seen from the two pro formas, the Job Costing Sheet for Renowindo records in detail all items that contribute to the specific order, and these costs are then computed and transferred to the Cost Summary Sheet.

To illustrate the costing of a job further, the following Job Costing Sheet and Cost Summary Sheet consider a job example 'Job ref. no. 0002' from Renowindo.

RENOWINDO LTD

JOB COSTING SHEET

Job Ref. No.:	0002	Job start:	12-6-2000
Customer Ref. No.:	6644		
Product Ref. No.:	DGD 45	Job end:	26-6-2000

Direct Materials Required:

Part number	Quantity	Cost/unit.	Total Cost
frame 12	5	£45	£225
window furn. 06	10	£12.50	£125
casement lock 133	5	£18	£90
glass	5	£20	£100
TOTAL DIRECT MATERIALS COST:			**£540**

Direct Labour Required:

Skill area	Hours	Hourly rate	Total Cost
Fitter	16	£20	£320
Glazier	20	£15	£300
Painter	12	£10	£120
TOTAL DIRECT LABOUR COST:			**£740**

Direct Expenses Required:

Category	Quantity		Total Cost
TOTAL DIRECT EXPENSES:			**NIL**

Overhead Requirements:

Indirect Expense	Quantity	Rate	Total Cost
Admin.	1	Contribution	£12
Factory O/H	1	Contribution	£36
Sales	1	Contribution	£20
TOTAL INDIRECT OVERHEAD:			**£68**

RENOWINDO LTD

COST SUMMARY SHEET

Job Ref. No.: **0002**

Customer Ref. No.: **6644**

Product Ref. No.: **DGD 45**

COST CENTRES	TOTAL COST (£)
TOTAL DIRECT MATERIALS	£540
TOTAL DIRECT LABOUR	£740
TOTAL DIRECT EXPENSES	Nil
TOTAL INDIRECT OVERHEAD	£68
TOTAL JOB COST	**£1348**

09-4

From examination of this worked example, it can be observed that the section totals on the Job Costing Sheet have been transferred to the Cost Summary Sheet, and both forms contain the same job, customer and product reference numbers to allow audit trails to be followed by both the organization accountant and an external auditor.

The job summary, showing the 'cost of goods sold' will be recorded in the trading and profit & loss account of Renowindo, and onto this figure will be added a mark-up, resulting in the computation:

Cost of Goods Sold + Mark-up = Sales Income (Price)

This computation, used for all jobs conducted during the financial year, will be the basis of calculations for profit in Renowindo's accounts.

A type of job costing that has not been considered so far might concern the way in which a voluntary organization has to not only cost a job, but also to ensure as far as possible that the situation relating to revenue and expenditure achieves break-even.

The following case study, 'The Essex Childcare Trust', considers the situation of costing and break-even faced by many organizations in the public and voluntary sectors.

NOT-FOR-PROFIT CASE STUDY: ESSEX CHILDCARE TRUST

The Essex Childcare Trust is a voluntary organization based in Basildon (UK). It is concerned with assisting disadvantaged children. The Trust contacted a specialist children's organization, 'Childmind', based in another part of the UK with a view to developing a two-day conference on 'Caring for Children from Disadvantaged Backgrounds', to be run on 6 and 7 June.

Although making a profit is not necessary, it is essential that the event breaks even. Therefore all costs incurred in setting up and running the conference must be covered.

The venue of the conference will be The Manor House Hotel in Essex near the M25 London Orbital Motorway. The hotel can accommodate up to 120 people, and can offer full conference facilities for up to 86 conference delegates.

Six expert speakers have been approached and provisionally booked to present papers on a variety of subjects from special educational needs to consumerism.

All of the speakers will require both fees and expenses to be paid, but because of the nature of the organization and the event, they have accepted much reduced fees and economy class expenses.

The following is a list of anticipated/estimated costs for the event:

☞ Special delegate rate for accommodation, inclusive of all meals except for the conference dinner = £86 per delegate per night

☞ Conference dinner on the evening of the 6th June = £33 per delegate

☞ Speaker fees = £400 per speaker

☞ Speaker budgeted travel costs = £520 in total

☞ Speaker budgeted general expenses = £480 in total

☞ Delegate conference pack containing conference papers = £25 per delegate

☞ Conference advertising budget = £2,000

☞ Conference administration and event organization = £5,600

☞ Advertising mail-shot to individuals, local authorities, voluntary groups, schools and colleges = 2,000 @ 60p each = £1,200

☞ Non-refundable hotel booking deposit = £1,300.

09-4

The anticipated charge for the two-day conference is £480 per delegate, fully inclusive of the conference, accommodation, conference dinner, and conference pack.

Financial management of the Trust is the responsibility of the Trust's Secretary/General Manager. She faces the following challenges with the conference:

(1) The requirement to break even for the Trust.
(2) Ensuring that the conference is fully attended.
(3) The ability to offer a number of free places to delegates from other not-for-profit organizations, providing that break-even has been reached.
(4) Ensuring high-profile coverage of the event from the media, e.g. by offering media representatives meals and accommodation where necessary.

The Essex Childcare Trust

Conference 6 – 7 June

Computation of Fixed and Variable Costs

	£
Delegate Costs (Variable Costs)	
Accommodation and meals	172
Delegate pack	25
Conference dinner	33
Total Variable Cost	**230**
Conference Costs (Fixed Costs)	£
Speakers' fees	2,400
Speakers' travel expenses	520
Speakers' general expenses	480
Hotel deposit	1,300
Advertising budget	2,000
Mail shot costs	1,200
Administration costs	5,600
Total Fixed Costs	**13,500**

The Essex Childcare Trust

Conference 6 – 7 June

Computation of Break-even

The equations to consider are as follows:

$$C = a + bq$$

$$R = pq$$

Where
C = Total costs
R = Total revenues
a = Fixed costs
b = Variable costs
p = Price per delegate
q = Number of delegates

Break-even will occur when $R = C$

i.e. where: $q = \dfrac{a}{p - b}$

Therefore:

Total fixed costs (a)	= £13,500
Variable cost per unit (b)	= £230
Price per unit (p)	= £480
Break-even delegate number	= $\dfrac{£13,500}{£480 - £230}$
	= $\dfrac{13,500}{250}$
	= 54 delegates

09-4

Having completed the break-even calculation, the Trust Secretary now knows that she needs to get 54 delegates to the conference, each paying £480. With a capacity of 86 conference delegates, if she gets more than 54 she will then be able to fund media costs and/or free places for other not-for-profit organizations.

Financial Performance

For any given situation, the break-even point can be calculated graphically by plotting costs/revenue (£/$) against the number of units sold. A graph similar to the following will be obtained:

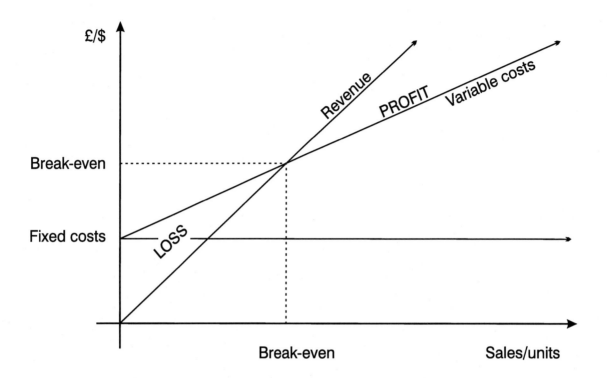

09-4-6 Managing Costs

The previous sections have dealt with costs which are relatively easy to

- ☛ Identify and calculate
- ☛ Apportion to work activities
- ☛ Monitor and control.

In our previous examples, we have looked at a sequence of manufacturing costs, but in reality, cost behaviour is frequently more complex and costs rarely behave in isolation from each other. In the Essex Childcare Trust case study, consider the impact of the conference on the following costs:

- ☛ Running the Trust's offices — increased electricity, stationery and other 'infrastructure' costs.
- ☛ Perhaps increased staffing costs through extra hours worked — either directly or as a result of having to complete 'displaced' work.
- ☛ Extra expenses for staff having to support the running of the conference away from the office.

www.universal-manager.co.uk

The break-even calculation is fine as it stands, but it is taken in isolation from the other costs to the Trust. Trustees have perhaps decided to stage the conference and the other costs (and the conference's impact on other costs) will be accepted — whatever they might be (presumably because they are incidental).

In today's intensely competitive business environment, more sophisticated approaches are required if managers are to manage costs effectively. In *Competitive Advantage* (1998), Michael Porter suggests that the concept of 'value chains' is essential to understanding cost. An organization's value chain is made up of its *primary* activities (which are essential to creating, making and delivering its products or services) and its *support* activities (without which the primary activities could not be performed). In Porter's model of the value chain (illustrated below) costs are assigned to the activity in which they are incurred and assets are assigned to the activity in which they are most utilized; and the costs of support activities are assigned across primary activities.

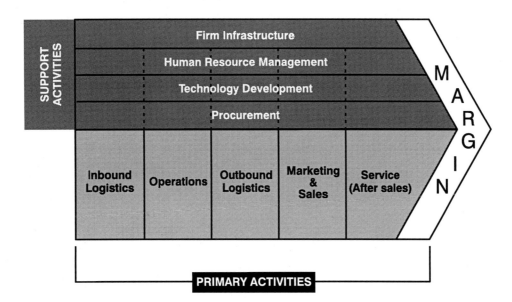

(Source: M E Porter (1985), *Competitive Advantage*, Free Press.)

Porter also articulates the concept of 'cost drivers' and lists ten of them:

- ☛ Economies of scale
- ☛ Learning ('resulting from improving know-how and procedures' over time).
- ☛ The pattern of capacity utilization
- ☛ Linkages (the impact flowing from how other value activities are carried out)
- ☛ Interrelationships (the way in which strategic business units work together, e.g. in shared activities)
- ☛ Integration (with supply of other value activities)
- ☛ Timing
- ☛ Discretionary policies (e.g. what level of service to provide)
- ☛ Location
- ☛ Institutional factors (governmental/regulatory drivers).

These cost drivers determine how the costs of value activities behave.

The effects of analysing costs in this way are:

☛ Managers have to understand costs in much greater detail — beyond the numbers and simple ratios.

☛ Accounting and financial reporting have to be rethought — the traditional reporting/account/budget lines will not suffice.

☛ Greater sophistication is required in financial analysis and modelling.

Further study of Porter's models is recommended for those working in a business environment.

 ACTIVITY 16

Identifying and analysing the cost of value activities in Porter's value chain is a complex exercise. For now, identify a discrete activity within your organization or department where 'value is added' to your organization's/ department's output. (By adding value, we mean increasing the value of inputs through some process which will reflect in higher value outputs in the view of a third party, i.e. we do not simply mean adding costs to the inputs.) The activity that you choose might be part of a manufacturing process, it could be labelling, packing/dispatching, sales order processing, contracting, a marketing or promotional service, and so on.

Write down the 'title' of the activity, and then list below it any of Porter's cost drivers which you think should apply to the activity. Note next to each whether you think that there is the potential to drive cost down in any of these ten areas.

Refer to Appendix 1 for a commentary on this activity.

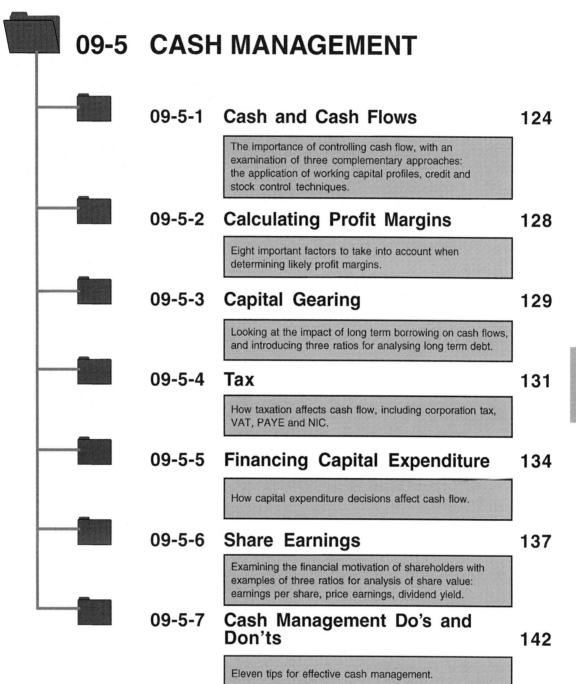

09-5 CASH MANAGEMENT

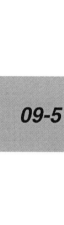

09-5

09-5 CASH MANAGEMENT

'Ah, take the Cash, and let the Credit go,
Nor heed the rumble of a distant Drum!'
(The Rubaiyat of Omar Khayyam, ed. Edward Fitzgerald, 1809-1883)

The need for cash and the importance of cash flow and liquidity are fundamental for an organization to run effectively in its day-to-day activities. Cash is literally the life-blood of the organization. Cash has therefore to be properly managed, as a shortfall in available cash may result in an organization's inability to meet its outstanding commitments.

09-5-1 Cash and Cash Flows

In accountancy terms, cash is the liquid asset of an organization. The amount of cash flowing into an organization, and the timing of this inflow compared to any outflows, is crucial in determining the solvency and ultimately the viability of an organization. Most organizations wish to remain viable, and a key to this future viability is the correct husbandry of their most liquid asset, cash.

It is self-evident that having too little cash can be extremely harmful to a business enterprise. However having too much cash can also have a negative effect on an organization, as money held is cash that is not working toward delivering the strategic objectives of the organization.

ACTIVITY 17

Obtain a copy of the Annual Report for your own organization. Look at the Balance Sheet and examine the total asset profile, both fixed and current, of your organization. Now calculate the percentage of total corporate asset that the cash balance of your organization comprises.

Where possible, talk with your corporate accountant and ask for the strategic reasons behind that cash asset percentage. (It could be a liability.)

Now read on.

Cash Flows

Any strategic planning or financial forecasting must ensure that the pattern of corporate cash flow is taken into account. The organization may deal in seasonal products, giving a skewed picture of major cash inflows, and therefore any cash outflows should be regulated accordingly. Particular financial decisions that can assist in the management of organizational cash flow will include decisions relating to:

- ☞ Working capital profiles
- ☞ The calculation of profit margins
- ☞ Capital gearing
- ☞ Corporate tax
- ☞ Dividend payments
- ☞ Capital expenditure programmes.

Working Capital Profiles

Working capital is the difference between current assets and current liabilities (creditors, bank short-term loans, dividends, interest, etc.). Each of these assets and liabilities will have a clear and important impact upon the financial health of the organization, as they can all influence the cash flow profile.

09-5

CASE STUDY:
RAINDROP PLC (3)

Raindrop PLC

(Refer to section 09-1-3 for background and data on this organization.) With regard to the example of Raindrop PLC, the situation described concerning the Net Working Capital shows that Raindrop PLC has been particularly cautious, with a 3:1 ratio of current assets to current liabilities in 1997/1998.

When the working capital is examined more closely, it can be seen that the cash balance alone covers approximately 50% of total current liabilities. It is of further note that other asset areas such as debtors and stock have to be closely examined in order that cash flow management is properly handled.

For example, the situation at Raindrop PLC concerning debtors is that on average over the three-year period 1997 – 1999, the debt collection time is approximately 80 days. (Whether this is good or bad can only be determined by benchmarking against the sector norm.)

If the creditor payment time for the same period is examined, the following is shown using the formula:

$$\textit{Creditor Period} = \frac{\textit{Creditors}}{\textit{Average Sales per Day}}$$

$$1997 = \frac{£148,000}{£2,624,000} \times \frac{365}{1} = 20.6 \text{ days}$$

$$1998 = \frac{£286,000}{£2,899,000} \times \frac{365}{1} = 36 \text{ days}$$

$$1999 = \frac{£494,000}{£3,666,000} \times \frac{365}{1} = 49.2 \text{ days}$$

This shows that Raindrop PLC is paying off its creditors in an average time of one month over the three-year period 1997 – 1999. What is now obvious in terms of cash flow management concerning debtors and creditors, is that Raindrop PLC is taking almost three months to collect cash from debtors while paying off its creditors in one month. There may be reasons for this but it certainly looks like poor financial management. Potentially more money could be leaving the organization than is coming in — a recipe for financial disaster!

Credit Control

Giving customers extended credit costs an organization money. It is up to managers to ensure that the credit zone is calculated in advance and strictly controlled. The converse of giving credit is receiving credit from suppliers. Managers should negotiate the most favourable terms possible, as the ability to receive credit from suppliers is the least expensive form of corporate financing. There is, however, an ethical dimension to 'taking credit' and the behaviour of large firms towards their smaller brethren in this respect has been discussed elsewhere.

PAUSE TO REFLECT

When would you pay a salesman's commission?

- ☞ On taking the order
- ☞ When the invoice is issued
- ☞ When the cash is collected.

It is imperative that managers work as a team in balancing credit relationships with customers and suppliers. The overall aim must be to obtain the best cash flow conditions for the organization while operating efficiently:

☞ Buyers need to obtain credit but maintain good supplier relationships to ensure that they can supply production when required.

☞ Production shouldn't demand raw materials too early (tying up cash in stock) or produce in excess of demand (tying up cash in stocked finished goods). However, production should deliver on time for the sales team.

☞ Sales teams need to supply products on time to customers and ensure that cash is collected promptly. They must accept that customers who don't pay, or pay very late, are not worth having. Sales revenue is required to fund buying and generate profit.

☞ Finance needs to support the three operations to ensure smooth cash flow.

☞ Managers in all departments need to work closely as a team to ensure positive cash flow and profit.

09-5

Stock

With regard to the current asset portfolio of an organization, it is important to consider policy with respect to stockholding. Stock, in financial management terms, is considered to be the least liquid of the current assets held by an organization. This is emphasized in the different weightings between current ratio calculations and acid test ratio calculations.

Stock holding usually has a monetary value placed upon it. However, sometimes the stock goes out of fashion, or stock is held in the wrong sizes, for example. Stock value may, in such circumstances, decrease in value.

It is certainly true that the time taken in converting cash equivalents to cash, compared to selling stock holdings, is substantially quicker. It is therefore imperative that stock management is seen in financial terms rather than simply in potential customer convenience terms.

A further aspect of stockholding is its relationship to cash flow. This is called stockturn, and shows the number of times the average stock holding figure is sold over a trading period (usually one year).

There are two accepted formulae for calculating the rate of stockturn (or inventory turnover). These are:

$$(1) \quad \frac{Sales}{Average\ Stock}$$

$$(2) \quad \frac{Cost\ of\ Sales}{Average\ Stock}$$

(The preferred calculation is the second formula.)

The rate of stockturn is highly significant in cash flow management, and will vary from industry to industry. For example, retail grocers will look for a high stockturn rate, while retail jewellers will expect a low stockturn. These differences impact on strategic pricing policies chosen by the organization.

 09-5-2   Calculating Profit Margins

The decisions made within an organization in determining profit margins will greatly influence its cash inflows and outflows. In determining the price to charge for a product or service, many factors must be taken into consideration, including:

☛ Competition — Is your organization a leader or follower in the marketplace?

☛ Exclusivity — Is your organization the sole supplier of the product or service?

☛ Distribution — Is the product easily available through recognized distribution channels?

☛ Fashion — Is your product subject to the vagaries of consumer taste?

☛ Demand — Is demand for the product outstripping supply?

☛ Taxation — Is the price to consumers/users affected by governmental taxation policies?

☛ Stage of product life cycle — Has the product just been launched, is it in the growth stage, has demand stabilized, or are sales now declining?

☛ Cost recovery — What price must be charged to recover costs of production?

www.universal-manager.co.uk

Many factors will influence the price an organization will charge for its products or services. Consideration of 'profit influencers' is essential in any rigorous financial planning process, as the need to generate some kind of profit is paramount in most organizations. We think of this profit as being the difference between the total revenue and the costs associated with generating this revenue; so anything that influences the revenue or associated costs will be considered as a profit influencer.

Whether the profit is gross, operating or net, the computation will appear in the trading and profit & loss accounts of the organization. (The calculation of gross and net margins was covered earlier in this dossier.)

 ### 09-5-3   Capital Gearing

Capital gearing or the debt burden of an organization is concerned with the long-term policy of financing — the choice between raising funds by long-term borrowing from financial sources beyond the direct control of the organization, or by raising these funds from shareholders.

09-5

As previously discussed, the liquidity of an organization is concerned with its ability to meet its short-term financial obligations. However, this ability in the short term will be directly influenced by the long-term corporate financial decisions concerning future funding. Where an organization relies heavily on long-term borrowing, not only will the amount borrowed have to be repaid, but there will also be a requirement for accrued interest on the borrowing to be paid at agreed intervals. These repayments will impact directly upon the cash flow of the organization as they constitute a cash outflow.

To examine the impact of large scale future borrowing, consider a personal future financing decision — that of obtaining a mortgage for a flat or house. The lender, whether a bank or a building society, will supply an annual mortgage statement which will summarize mortgage repayments and outstanding balance.

For example, consider a 25-year endowment mortgage of £85,500 taken out in 1995. The annual statement for the year ending 31 December 1999 might appear as follows:

Opening balance on 1 January 1999	£85,500
Closing balance on 31 December 1999	£85,502
Interest charges paid during year	£4,633

Financial Performance

There is a long-term loan commitment for 25 years, and during that period only the interest charges will be paid off. These might vary according to current interest rates, and at the end of the period the capital originally borrowed has to be paid back. The hope with an endowment policy is that the investment managers of the insurance company are sufficiently adept, and that the stock markets are sufficiently profitable, for the policy to mature at the end of the term with a value greater than, or equal to, the loan capital. Unfortunately, fund managers and stock markets do not always perform to the expected levels.

In business it is similar with regard to long-term borrowing. The organization commits itself to meeting regular interest payments and these will affect the cash flow. When the loan has to be paid off, the payment will affect the asset profile of the organization.

Capital Gearing Decisions

Before taking decisions on capital financing, a prudent financial planner would calculate projections of the key ratios. For capital gearing, these are:

- Interest cover
- Debt ratio
- Debt/equity ratio.

(Section 09-1-5 shows how to calculate these ratios.)

It is worth noting that decisions concerning the sourcing of long-term debt must take account of potential pitfalls, including:

- The requirement of lenders for security against the loan must be met from the asset profile of the organization. UK banks' favoured sources of security are fixed assets such as the equity in property and land, which is typically valued at the difference between any outstanding mortgage and two-thirds of market valuation. Debtors are sometimes considered as security according to the quality of customer and debt collection experience. However, it may be that the organization has already taken long-term finance from this source through factoring. A proportion of stock and work in progress can sometimes be used for loan security; but it is unusual for lenders to take intangible assets as security. Particularly for small businesses, banks will usually require personal guarantees from directors (which in turn may be secured against personal tangible assets such as property).

☞ Potential cash flow problems may occur if repayments are linked to forecast sales which do not materialize. Sales forecasting is separate and distinct from financial forecasting and requires a range of other considerations to be taken into account. It will draw heavily on past sales experience and data from marketeers. However, financial forecasting disciplines should ultimately be applied because the key is the amount of revenue generated — not the number of units sold. Salesmen under pressure to achieve unit targets frequently fall into one or both of two traps — one is achieving higher volume through discounting, and the other is to achieve higher volume through allowing excessive credit. Either trap will reduce revenue and profit.

☞ Cash inflows may need to cover not only interest repayment, but will probably also need to be sufficient to repay the capital sum.

☞ Should repayments not be met, the lenders may exert pressure which might result in ownership and control shifting to the lender.

09-5-4 Tax

Corporation Tax

Corporation tax is a UK tax on profit which often represents a significant outflow of cash and it therefore needs managing in two ways:

☞ Its calculation
☞ Its timing.

Its calculation is generally handled by specialists in corporate law and taxation.

Corporation tax is usually calculated on a organization's taxable income, rather than profit; 'taxable income' is defined in the UK by the Inland Revenue. The level of taxation varies according to the size of the organization, but it is about 30% for larger companies — potentially a significant cash outflow. Two items frequently encountered in annual accounts are:

☞ Profit before tax — shown on the profit & loss statement, this is the trading account profit before corporation tax is deducted
☞ Corporation tax liability — shown on the balance sheet, this is the provision for corporation tax that has to be paid. It is necessary since the amount can be significant, it has to be paid within nine months of the end of the organization's financial year, and the amount is frequently subject to adjustment by the Inland Revenue.

In considering this tax, there are basically two kinds of corporation tax which will be encountered:

☞ Advanced Corporation Tax (ACT)
☞ Deferred tax.

An organization becomes liable for ACT when it pays a dividend to its shareholders. ACT has to be paid within 14 days after the end of the quarter in which dividends have been paid. Dividends are generally voted on at the AGM and the timing of the AGM can be decided within limits by directors and auditors. This means that the timing of ACT can be managed. Generally, ACT is offset against the next corporation tax liability — hence its name.

Deferred tax arises because adjustments can be made, for example when an organization makes losses. Adjustments can be applied to past or future years in order to reduce the liability in the current year. In effect, the tax liability remains the same, but it is moved from one year to a subsequent year. The current year's corporation tax liability would be shown on the balance sheet as a short-term liability, whereas deferred tax would be shown as a long-term liability.

In terms of managing cash, directors and accountants can make a number of decisions in two broad categories:

(1) Those which affect tax liability. These will include how and where to report profit. For example, mechanisms can be employed in group accounts which optimize tax liabilities between profits and losses generated in separate companies. Also capital allowances play a major role in reducing this kind of tax liability. (Refer also to the section on depreciation of capital assets.)

(2) Those which affect the timing of tax payment. Bearing in mind what has been mentioned above, there are a number of actions which directors can take to manage the timing of payment. To delay payment of ACT, the AGM should be held as late as possible and dividends should be paid as late as possible. As much advantage as possible should be taken of deferred taxation.

In relation to both aspects, a firm's auditors should be closely involved in decisions.

It's difficult to avoid tacks!

www.universal-manager.co.uk

Value Added Tax (VAT)

Value added tax (VAT) is a tax on both goods and services received and goods and services supplied and is levied at various rates throughout Europe. For most organizations in the UK, it is usually paid to the HM Customs and Excise quarterly. Some goods and services are exempt from VAT, such as books and bank charges. An organization which supplies more 'VATable' goods and services than it receives will pay out VAT at the end of the quarter; and an organization which receives more VATable goods and services than it supplies will receive a refund of VAT at the end of the quarter. This situation helps organizations such as:

☞ Charities whose revenue is through cash donation (VAT is not charged and therefore there is none to pay to the tax man)

☞ Start-up businesses which might be making a loss (spending more than they are earning).

For most organizations, planning for quarterly VAT payments is vital for cash flow planning as they can face significant quarterly cash outflows. Such organizations include service providers who have to charge VAT on their services but do not purchase many VATable goods and services (because their main purchase is labour). Betting shops are another example because they cannot reclaim VAT and therefore always pay out VAT.

VAT is a complex area of tax in the UK and is best left to computers and accountants. However, in the context of cash management, there are two main points for managers:

☞ VAT receipts and payments must be included in cash forecasting

☞ Like Corporation Tax, there are some actions which managers can take to mitigate the cash flow effects of this tax. For example, quarters where revenue is high (and consequently high levels of VAT are collected from customers) are good quarters in which to make capital purchases because, depending on the financing arrangements, all the VAT can usually be reclaimed on the date of purchase. The converse (poor revenue quarters) does not necessarily apply.

It is always prudent for the non-financial manager to consult closely with an accountant in VAT matters. The final point to remember is that in the UK, the financial penalties in fines and interest are unrefined, severe and swift and they are dispensed by an extremely powerful authority — HM Customs and Excise. It is essential that managers ensure that their organization is punctual and accurate in both accounting for and payment of VAT.

09-5

Pay As You Earn (PAYE) and National Insurance Contributions (NIC)

PAYE and NIC are UK taxes on personal income which must be collected by an employer and paid to the Inland Revenue. This usually occurs on a monthly basis. The main issues for the non-financial manager are:

☞ These taxes are extraordinarily complex and get more complex each year, so the detail should be left to computers and accountants.

☞ Unlike VAT and Corporation Tax, there is little that management can do to mitigate the cash flow effects significantly. The cardinal rule, particularly for smaller businesses, is the same as for VAT — be punctual and accurate in both accounting for and paying these taxes.

When forecasting and setting wage budgets and targets:

☞ Employers have to make NIC contributions, which may be as much as 12.2%, in addition to gross wages each month.

☞ Annual payments have to be made in respect of 'benefits in kind' such as company cars.

☞ If staffing levels are constant, there will not be much variation in monthly cash flow. However, in some industries such as retail catering and hotels where staff turnover is high and seasonal, not only will cash flow vary significantly but administrative support must be planned for in payroll processing.

With respect to the audit process concerning PAYE and NIC, auditors will employ 're-performance' procedures. They will select a 'sample' of employees, and re-perform the calculations of gross pay, bonuses, overtime worked, PAYE deductions, and NIC deductions.

 09-5-5 Financing Capital Expenditure

Planned capital expenditure programmes to achieve future corporate objectives will have an immediate effect on the cash flow within an organization. Planning financially for the future will involve committing present resources as well as anticipated and forecasted future resources. As seen earlier, capital expenditure is tied directly to strategic corporate goals and objectives, and will depend on the product/market direction of the organization, and the 'project planning' capabilities within the organization. Investment appraisal (see section 09-2-4) should invariably be carried out.

There are several ways of financing capital expenditure and one of the main considerations for selecting the method of financing is the management of the organization's cash — the size and frequency of cash outflows. Other factors (timescale, ownership, etc.) are dealt with elsewhere in this dossier, but the cost of financing is also an important consideration. The following are some examples:

☛ Using capital reserves. Used when the capital finance is less than the organization's liquid reserves and leaves a balance for contingencies. Other financing options might cost more in interest than can be earned by savings and investments. Perhaps the assets have a relatively short life and will depreciate rapidly. Discounts may be obtained for immediate cash payment. An example might be buying computers (but not necessarily if a large new data system is being installed). In terms of cash management, single negative cash flow items are budgeted together with effects on tax payments.

☛ Loan finance. Used where the organization does not have sufficient liquid (or not committed) capital. A number of loan arrangements are available. In business, loans are generally secured against either assets of the business (plant, property, etc.) or personal assets of the directors. Loans can be straight lump sum loans, or drawn down in tranches (e.g. for projects) thus minimizing interest payments. Periods of repayment can be short to medium term, and costs can vary enormously. Factoring is one method where cash is advanced against the organization's debtors, but this method can be rather costly. Factors employ a variety of different methods of operating and this can make cash budgeting more complex. For example, a loan might be used for buying plant for the medium term.

09-5

☛ Leasing. There is a wide spectrum of leasing options ranging on the one hand from arrangements that are rather like loans to those that are like rental agreements. The former include 'lease-back' arrangements such as mortgages where an organization sells an asset, e.g. a property, to a finance company and then leases its use over a long period until repayment is achieved. There is also a range of hire purchase arrangements where a finance company purchases an asset and leases its use to the organization until repayment is achieved and ownership of the asset passes to the organization. Finally, there are lease rental arrangements where use of the asset is arranged over a fixed period, and at the end of the period the organization returns the asset to the finance company. The organization never owns the asset and it will only appear on the balance sheet as a liability for the term of the rental. Cars and office equipment are often financed in this way because they depreciate rapidly and quickly reach the end of their useful life.

☛ Rental. The organization rents the item from the finance company (or landlord) for as long as it needs to do so. An example might be office accommodation where a small firm cannot afford a mortgage or does not want to have to manage a property. Another example is where equipment is only required for, say, a six-month project.

☛ Equity finance. Raising cash by share issue is commonplace, but is used to finance long term strategic moves and/or growth. There is an immense variety of methods of raising cash in this way, and this is discussed in the next section. Every week, we hear of cash being raised in this way to finance corporate acquisitions.

☛ Grants. Organizations should never overlook the possibility of obtaining grants from local, regional, or central government, charities and other bodies. These are rarely available without strings attached and this may require a separate cost/benefit analysis.

All forms of financing affect cash management. The general rule is that the more complex the financing arrangements, the more complex cash management becomes (in terms of both forecasting and control).

 PAUSE TO REFLECT

Consider the premises where you work. Who owns them? What was/is the strategic reason behind the current ownership situation? Is the current arrangement the least costly option in the short term?

Whatever the reason for capital investment the decision to commit financing will affect the way in which:

☛ Profit is distributed
☛ Fixed and current assets are utilized
☛ Any financial shortfall is funded.

09-5-6 Share Earnings

Shareholder Motivation

Raising venture capital through share issue is a common method of financing organizations over the long term, e.g. for start-up, relaunch or major capital projects. Potential shareholders must have an expectation of profiting from their investment.

Shareholders subscribe to the shares of an organization for several reasons, the two most common being:

☛ Profit from an increase in the future value of shares purchased

☛ Potential income from dividend payments.

Profit from resale of shares is not usually a significant issue for managers within an organization. It only becomes an issue in exceptional circumstances, e.g. preparation for sale of the organization, acquisition or merger. In these circumstances there is usually significant pressure from the board room to squeeze every last bit of profit out of the organization, e.g. through delaying capital expenditure, tightening cash flow, asset sale or rationalization, decreasing stock holding, etc. The message for the individual manager is at the very least to be alert to what is happening with your organization's shares, and preferably buy some of the shares!

Another time when resale of shares is significant is if there is a change (increase or decrease) in confidence in the organization. Share valuation can change quickly, and with the advent of global internet share trading twenty-four hours a day, organizations can find that they lose control of their businesses very quickly. In this kind of situation, the effects are the same as the first example — directors tend to 'batten down the hatches' until stability returns. There is usually no direct cash flow implication for the organization (unless the organization's bank loses confidence because, for example, a loan is secured on an asset which suddenly diminishes in value). It is usually more of a serious restriction on the freedom of managers to manage.

Financial Performance

The dividend motive is rather different. It is the method by which shareholders ensure that directors operate a profitable organization; since the remuneration of directors is decided by shareholders at an organization's Annual General Meeting when dividend payments are also discussed, it is self-evident that the profitability of an organization and the fortunes of directors and shareholders are inextricably linked. Managers need to have a clear understanding of this linkage and should be aware of the main influences acting on directors.

Whether a dividend is paid or not is decided by a majority vote at the Annual General Meeting of shareholders. Usually, the vote is cast on the basis of the directors' recommendations after presentation of the Annual Report and Accounts.

Dividend payment is an internal financial decision which must take into account the effects of dividends on both the shareholders (owners), and future development of the organization that will require funding. Dividends are a cash outflow from the organization, but they are essential to ensure that shareholders stay with the organization rather than withdraw their funds and place them elsewhere.

It is therefore important to an organization to attempt to establish the rate of return on equity capital investment that will both satisfy the investor and enable the organization to retain sufficient profits to meet its short- and long-term financial commitments and fund its future objectives.

In the UK, there are conventions and legal requirements within the provisions of the Companies Acts that impact directly on the payment of dividends. For example there are aspects of finance that cannot be considered as being able to be distributed, including:

- ☞ Share capital
- ☞ Share premium account
- ☞ Any revaluation reserves.

Any dividend to be paid can only be paid out of 'Realized Profits', which are defined as follows:

'Realized profits mean those ascertained on a commercially prudent basis after making provision for historic cost depreciation; but note that where assets have been revalued upwards, the additional depreciation that arises as a result of the revaluation can be treated as an unrealized loss, and is not deducted in arriving at the figure for realized profits.'

There is clearly a knock-on effect of policies on depreciation and valuation of the asset base of the organization which will affect the profitability profile and future capital investment decisions.

www.universal-manager.co.uk

The dividend profiling of an organization will also be seen by potential investors as a barometer of organizational success, and therefore an investment opportunity.

As can be seen from daily stock market share value fluctuations, many investors are happy to move their capital investment from one organization to another in order to make short-term gains. However many larger investors, and owners, will look to future long-term returns and corporate plans and objectives.

The ratios that are influential in the eyes of present and/or potential corporate investors are as follows:

☞ Earnings Per Share ratio
☞ Price Earnings ratio
☞ Dividend Yield ratio.

Earnings per Share Ratio

The Earnings Per Share ratio shows the profits made by the organization during the year (after tax) in relation to the number of shares issued, and is calculated as follows:

09-5

$$Earnings\ per\ Share\ =\ \frac{Profit\ after\ Tax}{Issued\ Shares}$$

For example, if ABC PLC showed a profit figure after tax for 1999 of £2,250,000 and had a share profile of 4,000,000 fully issued and paid up ordinary £1 shares, the Earnings per Share would be as follows:

$$\frac{£2,250,000}{4,000,000}\ =\ 56.25\ pence$$

It must however be noted that not all of the Earnings per Share will be distributed to the holders of the four million shares. A proportion will be retained within the organization to fund the future development needed to achieve corporate goals.

Price/Earnings Ratio

The Price/Earnings Ratio indicates the value placed upon each share relative to the earnings achieved during the current time period, and is calculated as follows:

$$Price/Earnings\ Ratio\ =\ \frac{Current\ Market\ Share\ Price}{Earnings\ per\ Share}$$

For ABC PLC, the current share price is £2.66 per ordinary fully paid up and issued share. Therefore the Price/Earnings Ratio is:

$$\frac{£2.66}{£0.5625}\ =\ 1{:}4.73$$

The translation of this calculation is that investors in ABC PLC are willing to pay 4.73 years' earnings value for each share, or are willing to multiply the earnings value per share 4.73 times at current Earnings per Share values.

Dividend Yield

The Dividend Yield considers the dividend paid to the shareholders with respect to the current market value of shares and is calculated as follows:

$$Dividend\ Yield\ =\ \frac{Dividend\ Paid\ per\ Share}{Current\ Market\ Share\ Price}\ \times\ \frac{100}{1}$$

For ABC PLC the Earnings per Share for the period were calculated at 56.25 pence; however the bulk of this was retained within the organization to fund future strategic objectives and 16.5 pence was paid to shareholders as dividend.

The calculation therefore showed the following:

$$\frac{£0.165}{£2.66}\ \times\ \frac{100}{1}\ =\ 6.2\%$$

The calculation for ABC PLC shows that at present market prices and dividends paid, any shareholder who has invested in the organization is achieving 6.2% return on their investment.

ACTIVITY 18

(1)   Select one of the main global stock exchanges, e.g. London, New York, Frankfurt or Hong Kong, and identify one of the key indexes such as the FTSE 100 (London), Dow or NASDAQ (New York), etc.

(2)   Now select two contrasting organizations, e.g. a bank and a technology organization. Set up a spreadsheet on a computer and start to log weekly valuations of their stocks as reported in a newspaper (e.g. the Financial Times), on satellite/cable TV or on the internet. (Visit www.universal-manager.co.uk for links to sites.)

(3)   Set up your spreadsheet to calculate any of the ratios we have covered and note both how they compare and how they vary over the course of a convenient time period, e.g. three or six months. You might also be able to do this for the organization in which you work.

09-5

Summary

All of the above ratios which relate to the potential earnings opportunities for would-be investors can have a dynamic effect on funding availability and short- and long-term cash borrowing requirements.

09-5-7   Cash Management Do's and Don'ts

It is imperative that any organization manages its cash inflows and outflows prudently. With this in mind, profits made by an organization should be utilized within the context of the strategic plans and objectives of the organization. We have seen from the given examples that liquidity is more important, day-to-day, than profit. However, it is also important to retain a sufficient proportion of profits to reinvest, to enable future strategic objectives to be met. The control and management of cash will enable an organization not only to survive, but also to grow, providing that there is the correct financial forecasting discipline within the management of the organization.

A simple checklist of 'do's' and 'don'ts' for cash management should be noted:

- **DO** ensure that dividends paid strike a balance between rewarding the shareholders and achieving strategic plans.

- **DO** ensure that the organization has sufficient liquidity at times of anticipated cash outflows.

- **DO** collect outstanding debtor balances as quickly as possible.

- **DO** monitor cash budgets frequently.

- **DO** monitor debtor/creditor periods regularly.

- **DO** spend cash to budget (assuming revenues are on target) but maintain a prudent reserve.

- **DON'T** allow creditor balances to build up to such an extent that the most liquid assets cannot cover them.

- **DON'T** allow short-term profits to drive an increase in fixed costs such as salaries.

- **DON'T** assume that debtor/creditor periods remain constant.

- **DON'T** hoard cash (unless revenue targets are not being achieved) — make it work.

- **DON'T** withhold supplier payments unnecessarily — it will affect their performance (and you may need a favour one day).

APPENDIX 1

COMMENTARY ON ACTIVITIES

Activity 6

Galashields Gorillas SWOT Analysis

Strengths

- ☞ Now a Premiership team
- ☞ Substantial financial support from local authority
- ☞ Quality players — Premiership ability, therefore a substantial financial asset base
- ☞ Cash in bank
- ☞ Regular income from matches played.

Weaknesses

- ☞ Need to sell players (not key players?) to help pay for stadium
- ☞ At present, a substandard stadium which does not meet league requirements
- ☞ High expense profile compared to income generated.

Opportunities

- ☞ As a Premiership side, a greater opportunity exists to develop the merchandising activities at the club
- ☞ The club becomes a more exciting sponsorship opportunity for companies
- ☞ Increased income from charging higher entrance prices
- ☞ Increased income from a larger potential support base as a Premiership club.

Threats

- ☞ Inability to repay loan, therefore no new stadium
- ☞ Possible lack of success in Premiership, leading to relegation at the end of the season.

Activity 8

Here are some suggestions for points that you might have raised. This is a large and ever-changing area of debate and there are few right or wrong answers.

(1) (a) *Computers*

- ☛ Price — more 'computing power' for less money.
- ☛ Availability — increase in number of mail order offers. Little change in retail shopping opportunities. Internet shopping emerging. 'Ready to go' and 'Plug and Play' bundles more widely available.
- ☛ Size — greater variety of notebook computers available. Emergence of 'palm top' and hand-held computers. Generally the UK leads Europe in following the USA in the pattern of computer ownership, i.e. nearly all businesses and the majority of homes use computers — many with e-mail which is fast becoming the most popular form of correspondence.

(b) *Phones*

- ☛ Price — probably this has not changed much over five years, but the method of charging has become complex — sometimes involving 'free' phones. As with computers, more 'phone' for your money. Network access without contract.
- ☛ Availability — from an essential business tool, the mobile phone has become a mass market item with huge growth. Widely available in supermarkets, phone shops, and on the internet.
- ☛ Size — relatively slight change towards smaller, lighter phones with additional features.

(2) (a) *Marketing*

The primary focus for both personal computers and mobile phones has become the individual consumer — not business. The technological changes, which have driven down unit cost now, make these items mass marketing objects — using media such as TV advertising. However, manufacturers have to balance carefully their ability to supply the demand they create.

(b)   *Distribution*

In these rapidly-growing markets, a wide variety of distribution models can be supported:

- ☛   Products/services direct to consumer from manufacturers
- ☛   Independent and large retailers
- ☛   Build-to-order.

The challenge for the manufacturers is managing margins with a variety of distribution models (and hence a wide variety of margins/mark-ups to be maintained) while remaining competitive and retaining/gaining market share.

(c)   *Financial Forecasting*

Probably the biggest challenge is the rate of change of technology and the global nature of the business for both these products. Retail prices are rarely static for more than a week for a given product. Constant revision of forecasts and prudent revenue forecasting are likely to be cornerstones of the forecasting processes employed.

(3)   Obsolescence is not far away for many technology-based products. Their life-cycles are very short and therefore maximizing short-term returns is essential for any product. However, the merging of computer and phone technologies will require corporations to form strategic alliances. For example, hardware manufacturers will need to make fresh alliances with new software operating system designers — the old alliances will not suffice. Service providers (phone companies, ISPs, etc.) will be rationalized by the market and hardware manufacturers will need strategic alliances and/or partners in this field as well. The big players in the markets will ensure such alliances are global and not contained within national boundaries.

(4)   Whatever your organization, it is unlikely that you will remain unaffected by these changes. What do your colleagues think the impact will be?

Activity 11

Key Points for Board Report

- ☞ The 6-month position shows that the club is not viable without local authority finance. It also shows that there is little room for manoeuvre in cash terms. The Board should be advised to take the bank into its confidence immediately considering the cash facility that will be required. This may mean arranging a debenture over the club's assets with the bank.
- ☞ Directors should be fully aware of their fiduciary duties in this situation.
- ☞ The sale of players is a short-term expedient to raise cash. The result is likely to be poorer performance on the rink which will affect match attendance and game receipts beyond June. Other ways of raising finance are preferable.
- ☞ The club's bank facilities and collateral will probably need reviewing. It would be prudent to check the valuation of the club's main assets — land, buildings and players.
- ☞ Alternative sources of finance for the capital projects should be considered. Loan (from the bank or local authority), lease (through sale and lease back of property) and equity finance (through share issue to directors and fans) are strong possibilities. This would be preferable to sale of club assets, as these forms of finance will not adversely affect the club's ability to generate revenue. If one of the £¼M contractor payments could be financed in this way and sale of players postponed, a more viable future might be envisaged.
- ☞ The club should consider negotiating deferred payments and interest with the contractor, or possibly persuading the contractor to take part payment as equity in the club.
- ☞ The club must consider the ethical balance of raising prices tempered with a potential backlash from the fan base, who might see these financial moves as trying to 'rip off' the supporter. An opportunity should be made for the views of the fans and the concerns of the club to be aired and discussed. By communicating with the fans, the income base of the club, a more acceptable pricing policy may emerge through the process of consultation and communication.

Activity 12

A suggested solution to this activity is:

Growth Investments		*Replacement & Maintenance Investments*	
Project 1	£100,000	Project 1	£70,000
Project 2	£78,000	Project 2	£100,000
Project 3	£55,000	Project 3	£44,000
Total	£233,000	Total	£214,000

Cost Reduction Investments
Project 1   £40,000
Total   £40,000

Total: £487,000

This solution is straightforward in that it takes the investments in each category in the order that they are presented — in terms of net benefit. In other words in the area of Growth the first three projects have been selected; in Replacement and Maintenance it is the same picture; and in Cost Reduction (an area identified as a lower priority) it is the first investment opportunity that has been accepted. This method is sound, as it reflects planning based on the benefit-return of the investment. The choice is driven by the strategic aims and shorter term objectives. The majority of the investment is in the targeted area of Growth, with a similar investment in the identified area of replacement and maintenance. Cost investments are proportionally a lot lower, in line with the aims and objectives.

Other alternatives are possible — should Replacement & Maintenance Project 4 be implemented rather than Cost Reduction Project 1? (The financial manager will find it difficult to resist the opportunity to reduce costs.) Managers must take into account other factors such as resource availability and timing, but ultimately, they must be able to justify their decisions based on accurate financial data, and to demonstrate that they are working towards the achievement of the organization's objectives.

Activity 13

By carrying out a functional classification of costs in this way, we can produce a summary account for Renowindo 1998 – 1999 as follows:

Sales	£1,888,500	
Direct costs	£662,500	
Gross margin	£1,226,000	(65%)
Overhead	£516,500	
Net margin	£709,500	(38%)

Clearly, how we classify costs will directly reflect how we report the profitability of the organization. If, for example, the commission (£126,000) was treated as a direct cost, the gross margin would be reported as 58% — a significant difference.

Activity 16

It should be possible to identify the impact of all of Porter's cost drivers on the activity which you have chosen. This does not necessarily mean that there is the potential to change the current situation and drive costs down. Our general comments are as follows:

☞ *Economies of scale.* For example, what cost advantages can be gained from larger volume throughput? Consider how intangible (e.g. research or set-up costs) and capital costs might be amortized across a larger volume. Don't overlook the so-called diseconomies of scale where larger volume leads to complexity in systems, processes or management with consequent increased costs.

☞ *Learning.* It is more than likely that costs can be driven down in this area. Individuals and organizations are always learning from both internal and external sources, but organizations are notoriously bad at retaining their experience and knowledge. Consider what systems are in place to manage learning (e.g. knowledge management), but also consider the additional costs of implementing learning and its management.

☞ *The pattern of capacity utilization.* Consider seasonal variations and the effects of supply and demand. For example, government organizations administering tax demands will be operating at capacity during March/April each year, but not perhaps for the rest of the year.

☞ *Linkages.* How do other activities impact on the selected activity? One obvious example is IT maintenance. These days, the way in which IT systems are maintained impacts on most activities in an organization. IT maintenance might be sourced internally or from an external supplier. Quality systems should optimize costs in this area.

☞ *Interrelationships.* As previously explained.

- *Integration*. What is the best cost option: to source inputs internally or to outsource them?

- *Timing*. Do the costs of inputs vary over time? For example, is there a better time of year to buy materials?

- *Discretionary policies*. What organizational policies are in place which will affect the costs of the activity? For example, is there an environmental policy which reduces costs through recycling? Some environmental policies will increase costs.

- *Location*. Is it possible to move the activity nearer to its customers and/or suppliers?

- *Institutional factors*. For example, there may be local or national tax regimes which add to costs; conversely tax relief or grants may be obtained which reduce costs.

APPENDIX 2

USEFUL RESOURCES

Other (linked or relevant) Universal Manager dossiers:

Dossier 03:   *Planning and Controlling Projects*
Dossier 05:   *Managing for Knowledge*
Dossier 08:   *Business Planning*
Dossier 10:   *Managing Quality*

H M Coombs and D E Jenkins (1994), *Public Sector Financial Management,* Thomson Business Press.

R Doge (1989), *Concise Guide to Auditing Standards and Guidelines*, Chapman and Hall.

C Drury (2000), *Management and Cost Accounting,* Reinhold.

G Johnson and K Scholes (1998), *Exploring Corporate Strategy,* Prentice Hall.

M E Porter (1998), *Competitive Advantage: Creating and Sustaining Superior Performance,* The Free Press.

A Rice (1997), *Accounts Demystified,* Pearson Education.

M Smith (1996), *Strategic Management Accounting,* Butterworth Heinemann.

K Ward, S Srikathan and R Neal (1991), *Management Accounting for Financial Decisions,* Butterworth Heinemann.

Web Sites

www.universal-manager.co.uk
The Universal Manager support site includes a professional development area for finance plus useful book references and internet links.

www.cima.org.uk/tec/top.htm
Chartered Institute of Management Accountants (UK) site: mainly of professional interest to management accountants. Also contains a number of useful free downloads for students, managers and business planners.

www.ifac.org/Guidance/index.tmpl
International Federation of Accountants (USA). Mainly of professional interest to accountants and auditors. The General Standards area contains a range of information about auditing standards and related services.

www.hbsp.harvard.edu/free/index.html
Harvard Business School site. Contains a special area for accountancy and finance.

http://web.utk.edu/~jwachowi/wacho_hp.htm
University of Tennessee professor's homepage containing useful world wide web directories for 'discerning finance students'.

APPENDIX 3

NEBS Management Diploma in Management

NEBS Management is the Awarding Body for specialist management qualifications — committed to developing qualifications which meet the needs of today's managers at all levels across industry.

The NEBS Management Diploma in Management is a broad management development programme aimed at practising and aspiring middle managers. It offers a comprehensive, integrated programme of personal and organizational development.

Content

During the Diploma programme, a candidate will:

☞ Establish a Personal Development Plan
☞ Study theory and practice in the following key management areas:
   ☞ Managing Human Resources
   ☞ Financial Management
   ☞ Organizational Activities and Change
   ☞ Management Skills
☞ Produce a specialist Management Report
☞ Compile an Individual Development Portfolio.

Flexibility

The NEBS Management Diploma requires a minimum of 240 hours of study but can be completed on a full-time or part-time basis as appropriate. Many programmes will offer a mix of direct training, open learning and practical work-based activity. In connection with the Universal Manager series, the Diploma therefore offers the facility for learning in a variety of media including paper-based material, on-line resources and taught elements.

Assessment

Assessment of performance takes a rounded view of the capability demonstrated by the candidate in assignments and specialist tasks, in the management report and portfolio, and in interview.

Enrolment

The usual entry requirements are:

☞ At least two years' relevant management experience
☞ PLUS a NEBS Management Certificate, a Management S/NVQ at Level 3 or the equivalent qualification.

There are many Accredited Centres approved to offer the Diploma programme in the UK and abroad. Call NEBS Management on **020 7294 3053** for details of your nearest Centre.

INDEX

www.universal-manager.co.uk